Battling Boredom

99 Strategies to Spark Student Engagement

Bryan Harris

EYE ON EDUCATION
6 DEPOT WAYWEST, SUITE 106
LARCHMONT, NY 10538
(914) 833–0551
(914) 833–0761 fax
www.eyeoneducation.com

A sincere effort has been made to supply the identity of those who have created specific strategies. Any omissions have been unintentional.

Library of Congress Cataloging-in-Publication Data

Harris, Bryan.
  Battling boredom : 99 strategies to spark student engagement /
Bryan Harris.
    p. cm.
  Includes bibliographical references.
  ISBN 978-1-59667-166-9
 1. Motivation in education. 2. Effective teaching. 3. Academic
achievement. 4. Curriculum planning. I. Title.
  LB1065.H297 2010
  370.15′4--dc22

                                                    2010030235

10 9 8 7 6 5 4 3

Production services provided by
Rick Soldin a Book/Print Production Specialist
www.book-comp.com

Also Available from Eye On Education

The Passion-Driven Classroom:
A Framework for Teaching & Learning
Angela Maiers and Amy Sandvold

What Great Teachers Do *Differently*:
14 Things That Matter Most
Todd Whitaker

Rigor is NOT a Four-Letter Word
Barbara R. Blackburn

Seven Simple Secrets:
What the BEST Teachers Know and Do!
Annette Breaux and Todd Whitaker

Classroom Motivation from A to Z
Barbara R. Blackburn

101 "Answers" for New Teachers and Their Mentors:
Effective Teaching Tips for Daily Classroom Use
Annette Breaux

50 Ways to Improve Student Behavior:
Simple Solutions to Complex Challenges
Annette Breaux and Todd Whitaker

How the Best Teachers Avoid the
20 Most Common Teaching Mistakes
Elizabeth Breaux

How the Best Teachers Differentiate Instruction
Elizabeth Breaux and Monique B. Magee

Critical Thinking and Formative Assessments:
Increasing the Rigor in Your Classroom
Betsy Moore and Todd Stanley

Teaching, Learning, and Assessment Together:
Reflective Assessments
Arthur K. Ellis et al.

Engaging Teens in Their Own Learning:
8 Keys to Student Success
Paul J. Vermette

This book is dedicated to my wife Becky
for 18 happy years, and counting.

Contents

Part I **Strategies to Begin a Lesson** 1

Part II **Strategies to End a Lesson** 17

Part III   Strategies for Solo/Independent Work 33

Part IV   Strategies for the Whole Group 49

Part V   Strategies for Partners and Small Groups 67

Part VI   Strategies for Student Movement 83

Part VII   Bonus Strategies for Reluctant Learners 101

Acknowledgments

I have been fortunate enough to have spent years observing the skill, expertise, and energy of wonderful classroom teachers. I have been the recipient of their ideas, strategies, and feedback. My appreciation and admiration goes those classroom teachers who work every day to engage students in deep, meaningful, and relevant learning. I also owe a debt of gratitude to the talented school administrators who have allowed me to work in their schools. This book represents some of what I have learned from those extraordinary educators.

My deepest appreciations go to the following individuals who have helped make this project a reality:

> My wife Becky and my sons Andrew and Jeremy for supporting me and believing in me. They are my heart and I count it a privilege to go home to them every day.

> Of course to my mother, Edna Harris, who is convinced I am an artist but whose creativity is inspiring to everyone who sees her Candy Wrapper Creations.

> Bob Sickles and his team at Eye On Education for supporting me and believing in the value of this book.

> Julie Holdsworth, instructional specialist extraordinaire, for her ideas and encouragement. She is a true partner in this work and deserves much of the credit for some of the strategies found in this book.

> Dr. Frank Davidson, Dr. Barbara Wright, and the other talented and inspirational leaders in the Casa Grande Elementary School District who encourage me, listened to my ideas, and challenge me everyday. It is a privilege to be associated with them.

> And finally to Chad, who dared to tell the truth that sometimes, "School is boring!"

About the Author

Bryan Harris is the Director of Professional Development and Public Relations for the Casa Grande Elementary School District in Casa Grande, Arizona. He has extensive experience working with K-12 teachers providing staff development in the areas of brain-based learning, gender differences in the classroom, motivation, classroom management, and instructional strategies.

In addition to serving as a district-level administrator, he has served as a classroom teacher, instructional specialist, elementary principal, and adjunct university instructor.

He has obtained an advanced certification in brain-based learning from Jensen Learning Corporation and is a regular speaker at state and national conferences. He is currently completing his doctoral degree in educational administration from Bethel University in St. Paul, Minnesota.

www.battling-boredom.com
www.bryan-harris.com

Introduction

"We don't pay attention to boring things."
—John Medina, author of Brain Rules

"School is boring!" This was the exclamation from a teary-eyed student who was visiting my office for the fourth time in as many days. As a school principal, Chad was a regular client of mine. By client, I mean the type of student who seemed to have a standing appointment in my office. Formal learning didn't come easy to Chad. He struggled with reading, math, and just about every core academic content area. He lived for recess and physical education and yearned for an environment that let him explore, talk, laugh, run, and play. By third grade, Chad was already frustrated with a system that didn't meet his needs. He hadn't yet developed the coping skills that he needed to be successful in a formal learning environment. In my many talks with him, it became clear that he desperately wanted to be "good" and to do well in school. He wanted to be like the other kids and get good grades, complete his homework on time, and receive recognition for his efforts.

As I sat in my office that day with Chad, I started to reflect on his experiences and frustrations. I started to ponder on some important questions about the experiences of other students in my school. Not only did I want to find ways to help Chad succeed, I wanted to know more about the thoughts and ideas of other students in my school. How many other Chads were out there? After a few moments of thought, I turned to Chad and made a statement that both shocked and delighted him at the same time.

"You're right," I said. I then followed up by asking questions about his school experience, his successes, and what he found to be most frustrating.

The conversation that day with Chad started a mission of sorts for me. I went on to make it a personal goal to find out as much as I could about the perceptions of the students in my school. What did they find interesting? What was engaging and fun? What was boring and pointless? I made it a quest to help students like Chad, who out of frustration had the courage to speak what many students wish they could say, "School is boring and I'm only here because I have to be. If I could be somewhere else doing something else, I would."

Although this book isn't only about the Chads of the world, his frustration offers us the opportunity to look in the pedagogical mirror and reflect on some important questions. Starting the next day, I made it part of my daily interactions with teachers to ask, "What's fun today?" I would ask teachers about what elements of their lessons and daily activities were engaging, exciting, and motivating. More than one teacher would roll their eyes and retort, "Not everything can be fun, Bryan." I'd respond with a polite but persistent, "I know. Now tell me what's fun in your class today."

The problem of boredom is not new. Students have struggled for years to find meaning and true engagement in their school work. In 1984, John Goodlad wrote that boredom in school is "…a disease of epidemic proportions." Perhaps today more than ever our students are being vocal about their dissatisfaction with the way we do school. They are reporting that school work seems irrelevant, disconnected to the real world, and downright uninteresting. In 2006, the Indiana University School of Education released a report titled *Voices of Students on Engagement: A Report on the 2006 High School Survey of Student Engagement.* The findings are both startling and understandable. The survey of over 81,000 students found that 50% reported being bored in school every day while 75% report that they are bored because, "The material wasn't interesting."

Stating that some students are bored in class isn't necessarily headline news. The good news is that we know what causes boredom and we know how to engage students. The last two decades have seen the academic research on engagement and boredom offer numerous insights into how we can align classroom activities to battle boredom and engage students on a meaningful level. Teachers and schools that have made student engagement a priority see dramatic results. When students see the value in what they do and how they do it, they will come to see school as an important place that offers them meaningful growth and opportunities to discover their potential.

I wish I could report that Chad experienced a remarkable overnight turn around in his behavior and level of school engagement, but that wasn't the case. Like many students, he still struggled to find meaning and relevance in the academic content as well as in the teaching methods used by his teachers. We did see a slow change in some of his coping skills, but he still struggled to thrive in a system that wasn't designed for his needs. There are countless Chads in our schools and classrooms who yearn for school to be fun, exciting, relevant, and meaningful.

This book is written for teachers who want simple-to-use, ready-to-go, classroom-tested strategies to engage students. Battling student boredom starts with teachers making conscious decisions to engage students in meaningful ways. The effective teacher is constantly on the lookout for new, novel, and imaginative ways to engage students in the content and learning.

In order to effectively battle boredom, teachers should:

- Plan specific strategies, lessons, and techniques to engage a variety of learners. Teachers should incorporate specific strategies based on the needs of their students.

- Monitor the strategies being used and adjust to meet the needs of the students.

- Have backup strategies ready because not every strategy works equally well with all students.

- Demonstrate enthusiasm about the content being learned as well as the methods for learning and instruction. Teachers should exude a genuine belief that the learning and content are valuable and meaningful.

♦ Communicate the relevance of the content being studied. Students want to be engaged in learning that is relevant to their lives, interests, and future.

♦ Celebrate successes both big and small. Success at a task is motivating, exciting, and encourages students to continue their efforts.

■ What is Boredom and Engagement?

In my discussions with teachers about how to effectively engage students, it seems that engagement and boredom are a bit like art. I may not know exactly how to define it but I know it when I see it. In the context of the classroom, I have defined boredom as a temporary emotional condition marked by disinterest in the information, context, or events provided by the teacher that may sometimes result in inappropriate behaviors. Conversely, engagement in the classroom can be defined as a state of emotional and cognitive commitment or willingness to participate in the task or learning goal.

Engagement seems to be related closely to motivation, and like motivation, it is multi-faceted. Traditionally, engagement was defined and measured by student on-task behavior (Stronge, 2002). More recent research suggests that engagement involves cognitive, emotional, and behavioral dimensions as well (Fredericks, Blumenfeld, & Paris, 2004). For classroom teachers, it is easy to consider engagement as attending to the instructional activities of the class (Marzano, 2007). However, teachers must consider more than just student participation. A teacher must consider the tasks and activities that students are asked to participate in. The learning tasks themselves must be interesting and engaging. Eric Jensen, author of *Teaching with the Brain in Mind*, points out that if our students are bored, they are still learning. They are learning that school is pointless, that teachers don't care, that it's not worth trying, that that learning is a waste of time, or that school is irrelevant. Effective teachers take the time to consider how they might overcome these assumptions by students. They also take time to consider what students are truly communicating when they say "This is boring." When students communicate that they are bored, via overt statement, inappropriate behavior, or lack of participation, they might be saying:

♦ "I already know this, why do I have to do it again?"

♦ "I'm frustrated or confused."

♦ "I don't understand what is being asked of me."

♦ "I understand what is being asked, but I don't want to do it."

♦ "I don't see the value in what I'm being asked to do."

♦ "I've done this so many times, it's not interesting anymore."

Regardless of exactly how engagement is defined, why do some people get bored while others become engaged in learning? According to Dr. Mark Minter from Washington University, boredom is a temporary emotional state in which "The brain has concluded that there is nothing new or useful it can learn from an environment, a person, an event, a paragraph." The good news/bad news is that an individual rarely stays bored for long. The brain longs for input, exposure, stimulation, and interest. Bottom line: the brain doesn't seem to want to stay bored. That's the good news. The bad news is that if the teacher doesn't provide engaging learning opportunities, many students will find something that is engaging. And, like Chad, the new things they find to occupy their time may get them a one-way ticket to the principal's office.

■ How to Use this Book

This book was written for classroom teachers who want easy-to-use strategies to engage their students. It was written for teachers who want to meet the needs of students like Chad. However, even if you don't have many Chads in your class, this book still offers strategies that will meet the needs of all students, regardless of their learning style, past experience in school, or instructional level.

When designing learning opportunities for students, classroom teachers deal with **priorities** (standards and objectives), **processes** (activities and strategies), and **products** (the final outcome of student work). This book offers teachers process strategies that will engage students in meaningful ways so that the priorities are learned and products are thoughtful. Although all three, priorities, process, and products, inform and impact each other, the focus of this book is on process strategies that will engage students.

The strategies are organized into the following categories that are often used by teachers when designing lessons:

+ Strategies to Begin a lesson

+ Strategies to End a Lesson

+ Strategies for Solo/Independent Work

+ Strategies for the Whole Group

+ Strategies for Partners and Small Groups

+ Strategies for Student Movement

Although I have chosen to place the strategies into these categories, in reality, each strategy could be used in a variety of ways and in a variety of settings. I encourage teachers to experiment and utilize the strategies in ways that make the most sense for their students. As the strategies suggested in this book are implemented, it is important to take time to self-reflect in order to consider how the strategies might be adjusted, changed, or modified for future use. Therefore, the Resources section contains a list of self-reflection questions that should be used after new strategies are tried.

All of the strategies outlined in this book have been used with real students, in real classes, with real results. They have been tested, refined, and shown to be effective at engaging students. While not every strategy will be equally successful in every setting, the strategies here have been shown to effectively engage a wide variety of students. Teachers should pick and choose, adjust, and accommodate to meet the needs of their students. If you'd like real strategies that work with real kids, in real classrooms, then this book is for you. This resource was created primarily for classroom teachers looking for effective engagement strategies. However, administrators, academic coaches, parents, and anyone interested in battling boredom will find these strategies useful.

Part One

Strategies to Begin a Lesson

Agree/Disagree Statements

■ Overview

Few things motivate students to participate as much as the ability to agree or disagree with the teacher and/or with each other. This strategy allows students to express an opinion, consider the ideas and opinions of others, and discuss important ideas.

■ Step by Step

1. Prior to the lesson, choose three or more statements that can be made about the content.

2. After getting students' attention, instruct them that they'll need to signal agreement or disagreement with the statements that will be made. Signaling can take the form of standing, thumbs up, walking to a corner, or holding up an Agree/Disagree card. (See Agree/Disagree Cards on page 117.)

3. Make statements one at a time and ask students to signal a response to each statement.

4. After students have signaled their agree or disagree stance, provide an opportunity for them to discuss their stance both with those who agree as well as with those who disagree.

5. Example–For students studying characters and setting in a novel, create statements such as:

   "_____ has been the most influential character in the story so far."

   "The story would have ended the same if the setting was _____ instead of _____"

   "The (*best, most interesting, most disturbing, strangest*) part of the story was ..."

■ Tips and Variations

♦ After statements are made, students could be grouped according to their opinions.

♦ Remember to provide students with think time after each statement is made.

♦ Consider providing **Sentence Starters** to students in order to help them elaborate on their ideas.

♦ The **Agree/Disagree Statements** could be revisited at the end of a lesson or unit after students have learned more about the ideas and had a chance to elaborate on their opinions.

♦ Instead of using only agree or disagree statements, a student could rate, on a scale of 1 to 10, how much they agree or disagree with each statement.

Alphabet Summary

■ Overview

This strategy offers teachers a quick, easy way to pre-assess what students know or remember about a topic or content. Using pre-printed **Alphabet Summary** sheets (see Alphabet Summary on page 118) or 3x5 cards, the students brainstorm what they know or remember using the letters of the alphabet.

■ Step by Step

1. Provide students with an **Alphabet Summary** sheet or a 3x5 card with between one and five random letters written on them.

2. Provide students with a reminder about the content being learned.

3. Instruct students to brainstorm terms, words, or short sentences that begin with the different letters.

4. Provide between 3 to 7 minutes for students to list ideas.

5. Ask students to share their brainstormed words with partners or conduct a whole group discussion about the terms listed by the students.

6. Example–For students studying the solar system, provide students with an **Alphabet Summary** sheet as part of the anticipatory set portion of a lesson and ask them to brainstorm everything they know about stars, constellations, and the solar system.

■ Tips and Variations

♦ Place single letter cards in an envelope and have student partners take turns pulling cards out of the envelopes and relating the content to a word that starts with that letter.

♦ It is not necessary for a student to brainstorm a word for every letter.

♦ Consider combining the **Alphabet Summary** with the following strategies: **Give One/ Get One**, **Inside/Outside Circle**, **Wear-A-Word**, or a **Journal Response**.

♦ If this strategy is done using 3x5 cards, the teacher can collect the cards at the end of the lesson/unit, punch holes in them and place them together with loose leaf rings so students can use them to review.

♦ **Critical Thinking Connection**—Ask pairs of students to compare their lists with the purpose of indentifying missing information. Once missing information is listed, ask them to formulate a plan to find and remember that information.

Audio/Video Clips

■ Overview

Using audio and video clips are a great way to introduce topics, reinforce knowledge, or spark discussions. Interspersing clips into lessons will peak students' interest and provide a novel change from typical classroom activities.

■ Step by Step

1. Prior to the lesson, determine an appropriate audio or video clip that will meet the objective.

2. After getting student attention, tell them that they will be listening to an audio clip or watching a short video clip. Tell students specifically what to look for or what to listen for during the clip.

3. While the video or audio clip is playing, pause if necessary at times to point out important examples or ideas.

4. When the clip is finished, lead a discussion focused on the elements or examples from the clip on which students were instructed to focus.

5. Example–Download an audio clip of waves crashing on the beach as an introduction to creative writing for students. Ask them to consider the sounds they hear, the images that come to mind, and the words they could use to describe the experience.

■ Tips and Variations

◆ Consider showing a short clip and then doing the **Give One/Get One** or **Corners** strategy as a means for students to discuss what they have learned.

◆ The internet contains numerous resources with short, interesting, and well-done audio and video clips. A great place to start is http://www.teachertube.com.

◆ When used as an introduction to a lesson, short clips (between 30 seconds and 3 minutes) are most effective. Remember to connect the purpose of the clip to the objective being addressed in the lesson.

◆ Be sure to check with district's IT department in order to determine access and availability of video and audio streaming in your classroom.

Fantastic Facts

■ Overview

Interesting tidbits, startling statistics, and out-of-the-ordinary pieces of information have a way of focusing attention and sparking interest. Using **Fantastic Facts** to begin a lesson is an effective way to gain attention, motivate students to learn more, and to engage them in the content that will be addressed in the lesson.

■ Step by Step

1. Before the lesson, gather pieces of information about the topic that may seem odd, out of place, or particularly interesting to students.

2. After getting student attention, begin making the **Fantastic Fact** statements with phrases such as:

   "Did you know...?"

   "I found this really interesting..."

   "I'll bet you've never heard this before."

   "When I first heard this, I couldn't believe it..."

3. After each statement, offer the students the opportunity to discuss, expand, or elaborate on the **Fantastic Fact**. Encourage them to make connections between the facts and their own experiences or knowledge.

4. When all the **Fantastic Facts** are stated and discussed, clarify for students how the facts connect to the content being learned and encourage them to be on the lookout for other facts or pieces of information that they find particularly interesting.

■ Tips and Variations

♦ **Fantastic Facts** can be combined with other strategies such as a **Quick Write, Ticket Out the Door, Q and A Match,** or **Gallery Walk**.

♦ One option is to ask students to record or log their own list of **Fantastic Facts** about the content or subject being studied. These facts can be compiled for use in a report to peers, a written assignment, or used as small group discussion points.

♦ **Critical Thinking Connection**—Ask students to select one or more of the **Fantastic Facts** with the purpose of creating a mural, non-linguistic representation, or model that demonstrates the information.

Found It!

■ Overview

Most students need multiple exposures to words and terms before they become proficient in their meaning and use. This strategy offers students a low-stress opportunity to interact with important terms and helps them discover how words are used.

■ Step by Step

1. Prior to an assignment involving text or reading, provide students with a list of important vocabulary terms they will encounter in the reading.

2. Instruct students, either by themselves or in pairs, to scan the reading assignment and locate the key words. Ask them to list the page numbers, location on the page, or context (in a descriptive sentence, in a caption, part of a graph, etc.) where the word was located.

3. After students have had sufficient time finding key words, allow them an opportunity to discuss with partners or compare locations of words. Since the goal is to become familiar with the words and their context, it is allowable for students to use each other as a resource in locating words.

4. After students have had sufficient time to locate terms, provide them with accurate definitions or lead them to the correct locations or contexts. Clarify any confusion and show students how the words they have located will be used in the lesson.

■ Tips and Variations

♦ This strategy is particularly effective when students will be faced with difficult, complex, or highly technical terms. It allows them to interact with the words and ideas without the stress or worry of using the word incorrectly.

♦ Some students may benefit from being provided with both a listing of the words as well as the page numbers where the words can be found. Since the goal of **Found It!** is familiarity and not proficiency, provide as many supports as the student needs in order to be successful in interacting with the text and the words.

♦ **Found It!** can be used as a pre-teaching strategy a day or more before the formal instruction begins. This form of pre-exposure can be particularly helpful with English Language Learners or special needs students who benefit from multiple exposures to words over a longer period of time.

Personal Goals

■ Overview

Most students do better when they have a clear goal and understanding of the expectations and learning outcomes. The creation of personal goals helps to focus students on learning priorities and can cause them to listen differently during the lesson. When learning tasks are connected to personal goals, the learning becomes more relevant.

■ Step by Step

1. Provide a brief introduction to students regarding the content and focus of the lesson and ask students to brainstorm what they already know about the topic.

2. If appropriate, ask students to share with partners some of the ideas they brainstormed.

3. Ask students to consider what they already know about the topic as well as what they would like to learn. Help them to make personal connections and encourage them to ask unique and out of the ordinary questions.

4. Provide students with 3x5 cards, Post-it Notes, or sheets of paper to record their **Personal Goals.** (See Personal Goals on page 119.)

5. At various points during the lesson or unit, instruct students to pause, read their goals, and track achievement towards completion of the goals.

■ Tips and Variations

♦ Have students review goals at the end of the unit or lesson.

♦ Ask students to place written goals in a location where they will be seen often. Students could track and reflect on progress towards the goals through a **Journal Response.**

♦ Some students benefit from the use of a **Sentence Starter** when creating goals such as "I most want to learn about…" or "I am curious why _____ happens when…"

♦ The number of goals a student creates can be differentiated based on the needs of the students as well as the depth of the goals they write.

♦ **Critical Thinking Connection**—Ask students to thoughtfully self-evaluate the goals they have created. Ask them to rate, on a scale of 1 to 10, how demanding the goals were. Challenge them to create and track goals that will stretch them beyond their comfort zone.

Quick Draw

■ Overview

The opportunity to draw, doodle, or sketch as part of the learning process is motivating for many students. The **Quick Draw** strategy allows students the opportunity to be creative, have fun, and connect new and previously learned information.

■ Step by Step

1. Prior to the lesson, choose key words, concepts or ideas that students will encounter in the lesson.

2. As the lesson begins, provide students with a prompt, question, or a list of terms and ask them to create a picture that expresses their understanding of that idea.

3. Model for the students what a **Quick Draw** could look like so they have a clear understanding of the complexity and type of picture that is expected.

4. When prompted, provide students with time to create their own **Quick Draw**. These pictures do not have to be elaborate, overly detailed, or exact. Stick figures will work just fine.

5. When students have had time to complete their pictures (most students will complete a simple one in less than 3 minutes), provide them an opportunity to share their **Quick Draws** with partners.

6. After students have shared with partners, begin the lesson and explain how those pictures relate to the concepts or ideas being learned.

■ Tips and Variations

♦ This strategy could also be done as a pairs activity where each student adds something to the picture of another.

♦ Consider combining **Quick Draw** with a **Team Web**, **Give One/Get One**, or a **Snowball Fight**.

♦ As an option, at the end of the lesson or unit, have students add information to the **Quick Draw** they created at the beginning of the lesson. Have them compare, add additional ideas, or recreate the picture to demonstrate additional knowledge.

♦ **Quick Draws** can be done in learning logs, on scratch paper, in journals, on Post-it Notes, on 3x5 cards, on individual whiteboards, or as a part of note-taking sheets.

Quotes

■ Overview

The opinions, thoughts, or ideas of others will often catch the attention of students and help them to focus on the learning. Using **Quotes** as a tool to introduce a topic is a great way to spotlight their attention on important ideas.

■ Step by Step

1. Prior to the lesson, select one or more **Quotes** that directly relate to the topic being presented.

2. Display the **Quote(s)** and prompt students to consider what they think about it. Allow them think time to consider their thoughts. Some teachers prefer to ask students to write down their thoughts or list key words that describe their opinion.

3. Provide students with some information and context about the **Quote**, the author, and any other background that may help them to better form an opinion.

4. When prompted, ask students to share their thoughts of the quote with their partners.

5. After students have had sufficient time to share with their partners, gain their attention and explain how the **Quote(s)** relate to the topic being studied.

■ Tips and Variations

♦ Conduct an Internet search for "quotes for teachers" and you'll find dozens of sites that provide **Quotes** from famous personalities that can be directly linked to content.

♦ If appropriate for the age level, consider using **Quotes** that take a controversial stance or one where students will have a clear opinion.

♦ After the **Quote**(s) are shared, students could participate in a **Line Up**, **Corners**, or **Journal** assignment in order to share and expand their ideas.

♦ While sharing with partners, certain students may benefit from the use of **Sentence Starters** (see Sentence Starters on page 132) to help initiate discussions.

Rank It

■ Overview

This strategy asks students to consider and rank, on a scale of 1 to 10, their understanding of key terms, ideas, or concepts that will be presented in the lesson.

■ Step by Step

1. Provide each student with a **Rank It** form. (See Rank It on page 120.)

2. Display a listing of the key terms or concepts that will be presented in the lesson.

3. Lead students to read each of the words listed and think about what they know about the words.

4. Provide students with pronunciations if needed, but do not provide definitions or examples. Explain to students that the goal of **Rank It** is to think about what they already know about the terms.

5. Provide students with an explanation of the scale they will use to show how much they know about the words. Students will respond with a number between 1 and 10 to indicate their understanding of the words. A rank of 1 to 3 will indicate little understanding of the word, a rank of 4 to 7 will indicate moderate understanding while a rank of 8 or more will indicate a higher level of understanding.

6. Lead students to rank their knowledge of each word.

■ Tips and Variations

♦ Consider combing **Rank It** with **Content Nameplates**.

♦ Clarify for students what the 1 to 3, 4 to 7, and 8 to 10 rankings may mean by explaining that a low ranking may mean that the word is recognized, but can not be defined. A moderate ranking may mean that the student can provide a brief, but incomplete definition. An 8+ ranking may mean that the student can both define the term and provide an explanation.

♦ Since the goal is a simple pre-assessment of student knowledge, there may not be a need to challenge students who may provide a ranking that is higher than expected. At this point, there is no need for students to prove their knowledge.

♦ **Critical Thinking Connection**—Have students keep the **Rank It** forms and compare their rankings before and after the lesson. Ask them to explain, update, or modify their rankings based on new learning.

Snap Shot

■ Overview

Students are typically attracted to the pictures, captions, graphs, and diagrams of a text, book, or handout. This strategy allows them to first capture information from those visual sources before being required to use the information or have a discussion.

■ Step by Step

1. Before the lesson, determine an appropriate source (text, handout, website, poster, word wall, etc.) of information about the topic being studied. Determine if students will participate in **Snap Shot** with partners, small groups, or by themselves.

2. Distribute the resources and provide time for students to interact with the resource to get an overall sense of the topic, key words, or information.

3. As an analogy, tell students that they are going to have their brains take a rough "**Snap Shot**" of the information before they learn more. Tell them that they do not need to read every word, but rather get little bits of information from different sections of the source.

4. After a few minutes of flipping through pages and interacting with the resources, have the students stop and summarize what information they have gathered. They could summarize this information by compiling a list of key words, using Post-it Notes to tag important pages, or by having a discussion with partners or small groups.

5. After students have had sufficient time to develop their **Snap Shot**, discuss, and/or use the information in a partner discussion, gain their attention and lead a discussion about how the information they have gathered is related to the objective and focus of the lesson.

■ Tips and Variations

- ♦ Consider combining **Snap Shot** with **Coded Reading**, **Mind Mapping**, or a **Team Web**.

- ♦ Provide several different sources of information (a stack of library books on a topic, for example) and ask students to use those resources to determine important ideas to share with partners or small groups.

- ♦ If students compile information from their **Snap Shots**, gather that information for use later in the unit or lesson. For example, after students have learned more about the topic, hand back their original **Snap Shots** and ask them to add, extend, or compare the before and after learning.

Stories

■ Overview

Students of all ages, even if they won't all admit it, love a good story. Although teachers typically think of story-telling as something that is done only with younger students or in reading class, stories can add a powerful and motivating element to any content area, regardless of the age of the students.

■ Step by Step

1. Prior to the lesson, brainstorm what stories might best complement the objectives of the lesson. Often, curricular guides contain ideas and suggestions for stories.

2. Tell students that they will be listening to a story. If appropriate, tell them specifically what to listen for when they hear the story.

3. Read or tell the story.

4. After the story, tell students how the story connects to the content being learned.

5. Example–"Students, to start our lesson today I want to read you a story about a boy who didn't quite understand certain phrases and words that his parents and teachers used. As you hear the story, think if you've ever heard these phrases and been confused like the boy in the story." Read *Parts* by Tedd Arnold.

■ Tips and Variations

♦ The story doesn't need to be long, overly complicated, or detailed to be effective at making connections for students nor does the story need to be original. Children's books are a great place to start.

♦ Stories of individuals who have overcome adversity have a strong appeal to students, particularly those who struggle in school.

♦ Stories do not always have to have a strong, dramatic, or moral element to be effective. Humorous stories are often the easiest way to begin.

♦ For help on finding good stories, consult the school or community librarian. Provide them with the content you'll be teaching and ask them to help you find a story that will engage your students.

♦ **Critical Thinking Connection**—Ask students to relate the key ideas of the story to their own personal experiences. Lead them to make connections between the moral of the story and their own lives.

3 Things Cards

■ Overview

Students enjoy expressing their opinions but are sometimes reluctant to do so in class because they are unsure of how their ideas will be received by the teacher or their peers. This strategy offers students the chance to express their opinions about a variety of topics in a safe setting.

■ Step by Step

1. Prior to the lesson, brainstorm a list of words, terms, or ideas that students will encounter in the learning. Write each of those terms on a separate 3x5 card.

2. As students enter the class, hand each a card with a term on it. Not every student needs to get a unique term, but it helps if there are numerous terms circulating among the students.

3. When prompted, instruct students to brainstorm three things they know, believe, or think about the term that is listed on their card. It helps for the teacher to model for the students the kinds of ideas they could brainstorm.

4. Instruct students to share their three ideas with partners. If appropriate, have students with similar or identical cards find each other and share their ideas.

5. Example–To introduce a lesson on gravity, distribute cards with following terms listed: *force, pull, earth, moon, atmosphere, space, mass, Newton, tides, weight, law,* etc.

■ Tips and Variations

♦ This strategy can be used at the beginning of the school year to help establish the norms and rules in the classroom. Distribute cards such as *kindness, helpfulness, fairness, sharing, homework, motivation, preparedness,* etc. and ask students to consider what they believe about those ideas.

♦ Consider combining **3 Things Cards** with **Move and Touch, Card Sort, Fish Bowl,** or **Quiz Show.**

♦ Consider having students write their three ideas on each card and collect them after the lesson. When the unit is over or when it is time to review for an assessment, redistribute the cards and ask students to add three more things they know about the concept.

Ticket In the Door

■ Overview

Effective teachers know it is important to get students involved in a learning task from the very beginning on the lesson. This strategy provides students with a tangible, clear task but it also allows them the opportunity to become an "expert" in one of the ideas that will be presented in the lesson.

■ Step by Step

1. As the lesson begins, give each student a Post-it Note or 3x5 card with a key word, idea, or concept listed on it.

2. Tell students that they will become experts on the term or idea listed on the card. Explain that an expert not only knows how to define or explain an idea but they can also share examples, give characteristics, and answer questions about the concept.

3. Provide students with time to find or share definitions, characteristics, or key words associated with the term on their card.

4. After students have spent time adding ideas, definitions, and examples on their 3x5 cards, instruct them to place the cards on their desks.

5. Tell students to listen carefully as the lesson begins because when they hear their term talked about, they'll be asked to share some of what they know.

6. Begin the lesson on the topic(s), pausing at various points to ask students to share what they have listed on their 3x5 cards.

■ Tips and Variations

♦ Combine **Ticket In the Door** with a **Give One/Get One, Gallery Walk,** or **Found It!**

♦ If necessary, list both the term and the definition on the cards. Students could use their cards to create **Flash Cards 2.0** or in combination with **Teach One, Guess It**.

♦ It is not necessary to have a separate term for every student in class. While each student should have their own 3x5 card, multiple students could become experts on the same idea.

What's in the Bag?

■ Overview

This strategy incorporates the power of suspense and novelty to garner student attention. It involves only a simple paper bag, an object that can fit in that bag, and student curiosity to be effective.

■ Step by Step

1. Prior to the lesson, select a tangible, physical object that relates to the topic being presented. Before students enter class, place the object in the bag.

2. As the lesson begins, tell students that you have placed an object in the bag that directly relates to the objective of the lesson.

3. Tell students the objective and provide think time to consider what the object could be placed in the bag.

4. Lead the class in a question and answer session where students take turns guessing what the object could be. Consider using the **20 Questions** strategy during this time. If students seem stumped, provide some clues or respond to guesses with, "You're cold" or "You're red hot" statements.

5. Once a student has correctly guessed the object or the students seem stumped, show them the object and explain how the object relates to the lesson.

■ Tips and Variations

♦ As an option, ask students how they think the object relates to the lesson without telling them directly.

♦ Sometimes an odd association can be created between an object and the content being studied. For example, when studying whole to part fraction concepts, bring in an orange to display how one whole object can be divided into parts.

♦ **Critical Thinking Connection**—Consider asking students to think of items that could have gone into the bag that relate to the objective. Ask students to provide a justification for an item and explain how it relates to the lesson being learned. Sometimes students will think of excellent examples that can be used in later lessons.

Part Two

Strategies to
End a Lesson

Absent Student

■ **Overview**

This strategy provides students an opportunity to summarize their understanding of the central points of the lesson or topic. Students are asked to discuss and/or write about the main points of the lesson for a particular audience—in this case, that audience is an imaginary (or real) student that was absent from the lesson.

■ **Step by Step**

1. Provide students with an opportunity to think about the objectives of the lesson or unit. If appropriate, provide them with time to work with a partner or small group to share ideas or summarize their thoughts.

2. Give each student a 3x5 card, a Post-It Note, a piece of paper, or a journal.

3. Instruct them that they will be writing a letter or short note to a student that missed the day's lesson.

4. Provide time for students to brainstorm about what they will write. If needed, have students complete a **Gallery Walk** or **Send-A-Spy** to get additional ideas.

5. Provide students with writing time, pausing at intervals, to check progress and ask students to share their ideas with others.

6. Collect the notes as a **Ticket Out the Door**.

■ **Tips and Variations**

♦ Some students will benefit from the use of a **Sentence Starter** to begin the note to the absent student. For example, students may begin the note with

"Dear _____,

Today in science we learned about _____.

Three important things you'll want to know about _____ are…"

♦ Teachers can differentiate this strategy by offering some students the opportunity to list key words, complete a **Quick Draw** with labels, create a **Mind Map**, or use a **My Top 10 List** as a resource.

♦ This strategy is also effective with partners and small groups. In those cases, this strategy can be used to brainstorm ideas.

♦ **Critical Thinking Connection**—As students write their letters, ask them to prioritize the learning for the recipient of the letter. Students could include a paragraph in the letter that lists, in order of importance, the content that may be the most difficult to recall, practice, or explain.

Circle, Triangle, Square

■ Overview

This strategy asks students to think about the lesson or content from three different perspectives—what they are still thinking about (circle), three things they have learned (triangle), and what they agree with (square).

■ Step by Step

1. Provide each student with a 3x5 card, a sheet of paper, or a Post-It Note.

2. Have students draw a circle, triangle, and square. Ask them to separate the shapes by some space so there is room to write in or next to the shapes.

3. Tell students that they will be writing key words, short sentences, or examples next to each of the shapes.

4. Next to the circle, ask students to write something about the content or lesson that is still going around in their mind. This can be something they haven't quite totally grasped or something they are still thinking about.

5. Next to the triangle, have students write three things they learned.

6. Next to the square, students write something about the lesson or content that "squares" with them. That is, something they agree with, understand, or believe.

■ Tips and Variations

♦ Remember to provide students enough time during the end of the lesson to think and reflect about the content before they start to write. If the time is rushed, they'll think more about getting the task done than providing thoughtful responses.

♦ This strategy can be used as a **Ticket Out the Door**, included in a **Journal**, as part of a **Snowball Fight**, or collected over time to demonstrate growth of understanding.

♦ See Circle, Triangle, Square on page 121 for a reproducible to use with students.

♦ **Critical Thinking Connection**—Ask students to review the information from the triangle in order to create an illustration that demonstrates their understanding of the idea.

Journal Response

■ Overview

The use of journals can provide students with a chance to express opinions, thoughts, and ideas in a safe, creative format.

■ Step by Step

1. Provide each student with a journal. (Consider providing each student with a note-book that can be personalized and used for an extended period of time.)

2. Prompt students to think about the content or main objectives of the lesson. If appropriate, offer them the opportunity to have a partner discussion or to review notes, written materials, or books.

3. Give students a specific topic, question, or scenario and provide think time and/or an opportunity to share ideas with a partner.

4. Instruct students to respond to the question or prompt in their journal.

■ Tips and Variations

- ♦ The quality of journal responses can be strengthened with the use of **Sentence Starters** or **Outcome Statements**.

- ♦ For students who struggle with topics or ideas to write about, consider beginning with **Coded Reading**, **Give One/Get One**, or **Consultation.**

- ♦ Teachers can increase the likelihood of thoughtful, reflective responses from students by ensuring that feedback is provided in a timely and consistent basis.

- ♦ **Journal Responses** can be brief and variations can include listing acronyms, describing characteristics, asking questions, adding a **Quick Draw**, or writing a summary.

Keepers and Wishers

■ Overview

This strategy offers the teacher a glimpse into which terms, ideas, or concepts students have grasped. By labeling ideas as either a **Keeper** or a **Wisher**, students indicate which concepts they think they are likely to recall and which ones will need to be revisited in a follow up lesson.

■ Step by Step

1. Provide each student with two Post-It Notes.

2. Prior to the end of the lesson, create a chart with two columns. One labeled **Keepers** and the other **Wishers**.

3. Provide students with time to review the key ideas and concepts from the lesson. If necessary, ask students to discuss their thoughts with a partner.

4. Explain to students that they will write one idea, term, or sentence on each of the Post-It Notes. Instruct them to write a small K at the top of one and a small W on the other.

5. Tell students that the K stands for **Keepers**. On the *K* Post-It Note, they will write something from the lesson that they will keep, or remember. On the *W* Post-It Note, which stands for **Wishers**, they will write the term, concept, or idea that they wish they knew more about. That is, on the W Post-It Note, students should list ideas that they are unable to adequately or fully explain.

6. Lead students to take their K and W Post-It Notes and place them in the corresponding columns on the chart.

■ Tips and Variations

♦ One option is to use a handout with the two **Keepers and Wishers** columns. Ask students to list key words or ideas under each column and collect as a **Ticket Out the Door**. (See Keepers and Wishers on page 122.)

♦ When reading and analyzing the information students have written on the **Keepers and Wishers** Post-It Notes, look for commonalities in student responses. Pay close attention to those key ideas or concepts that students fail to include as **Keepers**.

♦ During a follow up lesson, consider distributing the Post-It Notes as a **Ticket In the Door**.

Letter to Self

■ Overview

This is a novel strategy that provides the students with a unique audience for their writing—themselves. Since the primary audience and recipient of the letter is the student writing it, there is a level of safety and security that allows the student to focus on their content learning without getting overly concerned about who will be reading the letter.

■ Step by Step

1. Provide students with a sheet of paper and a letter-sized envelope.

2. Tell students that they will be writing a letter to themselves that will outline what they know, understand, and still need to know about the topic being studied.

3. Let them know that it will be a true letter to self and that no one else will read it.

4. Ask students to summarize what they know about the unit of study and to make the letter personal by including anything that they need to do in order to better understand the topic.

5. After students have written the letter and sealed it in the envelope, collect the letters and let them know that they will receive the letter back at some unknown time in the near future.

■ Tips and Variations

♦ Some teachers have chosen to have students complete the **Letter to Self** at the beginning of a unit of study and then deliver it to them at the end of unit so they can see how much they have learned.

♦ Some students will benefit from the use of **Sentence Starters** to help them begin the letter.

♦ If school funds permit, consider sending the letters in the mail. Students love to get mail and will likely share the letter with their family

♦ When this strategy is regularly used, students can collect and compile their letters to get a long-term view of the learning that has taken place.

♦ See Letter to Self on page 123 for a reproducible for students to use.

♦ **Critical Thinking Connection**—When students are writing their letters ask them to include certain self-reflection verbs such as *defend, justify, support, and compare.*

Outcome Statements

■ Overview

This strategy allows students the opportunity to critically process and think about the content or information in a novel manner. Students are encouraged to consider the process of learning in addition to the content or information that was learned.

■ Step by Step

1. Instruct students to think about and reflect on what they know or have learned about the topic. If needed, provide them with a listing of key words, topics, big ideas, or questions.

2. Explain that students will be shown or given an **Outcome Statement** and that their job is to finish the sentence based on what they know or understand about the topic.

3. Provide students with choices of which statements they can finish and provide think time for them to consider their response.

4. Ask students to share their **Outcome Statements** with a partner.

5. Examples of **Outcome Statements** include:

    "I was surprised by…"

    "I am clearer about…"

    "I wish I knew more about…"

    "One thing I can explain clearly is…"

■ Tips and Variations

♦ Consider combining **Outcome Statements** with a **Journal Response**, **Ticket Out the Door**, or **Give One/Get One**.

♦ See Outcome Statements on page 124 for a list of additional **Outcome Statements.**

♦ When this strategy is used frequently, students may have a tendency to choose the same **Outcome Statements** each time they are asked to reflect. If that happens, consider randomly assigning the statements or use them as **Envelope Questions**.

Pass It

■ Overview

When students are asked to self-select important ideas and key questions, there is an increased likelihood that they'll be engaged in the lesson. This strategy offers students the opportunity to determine their own key learning from the lesson as well as see what other students have determined was important.

■ Step by Step

1. Provide students with three Post-It Notes or 3x5 cards.

2. Prompt students to think about the main objective(s) of the lesson. Provide think time and, if appropriate, the opportunity to debrief with a partner.

3. Instruct students to write one thing they learned on each card or sticky note. (Three cards = three things they learned.)

4. Once they have written the fact, term, or idea on each card, collect the cards.

5. After all the cards have been collected, shuffle them and give each student three random cards.

6. When students have their new cards, they read what was written and create a question that could be answered by the fact/information that was provided on the card.

■ Tips and Variations

◆ One option is to give each student just one to two cards and hold the others for an introductory activity during a follow up lesson.

◆ These cards could be used to review with partners or could be given back to the original student.

◆ The cards could be collected as a **Ticket Out the Door**, used in conjunction with a **Partner Pretest**, or as a **Card Sort**.

◆ **Critical Thinking Connection**—Lead pairs or small groups of students to prioritize and organize the information on the cards according to criteria such as *easiest to recall*, *most difficult to explain*, or *most likely to be on a test*.

Postcard to a Friend

■ Overview

This novel strategy allows students to summarize their learning for the purpose of communicating to a friend. The power is in the fact that students have a specific purpose for the writing and are provided with a short, easy-to-follow format.

■ Step by Step

1. Provide students with a blank postcard or a paper cut in the size and shape of a postcard.

2. Instruct students that they will be writing a **Postcard to a Friend** about the content or topic that was presented in the lesson.

3. Tell students that most postcards only have enough space for a few lines so they will need to summarize their learning in a brief, understandable way for their friend.

4. Provide students with think time and between 3 to 5 minutes to write their postcard. If appropriate, ask students to share their ideas with partners or provide a **Sentence Starter**.

5. Collect the postcards.

■ Tips and Variations

♦ An option is to have students write a postcard to themselves (similar to a **Letter to Self**) and then send those to the students as they prepare for an assessment.

♦ This strategy could be differentiated easily by asking students list key words, draw a picture, copy a text selection, or working with a partner instead of writing in complete sentences.

♦ The postcards could be used as part of an introduction to a follow up lesson, collected and used as a test review tool, or given out randomly to students as part of a **Give One/Get One** activity.

Press Conference Talking Points

■ Overview

When politicians, celebrities, athletes, and other public figures prepare for press conferences, they often prepare a list of talking points to help get their message across to their audience. This strategy uses that concept to help students determine talking points about the lesson or unit that was studied.

■ Step by Step

1. Inform students that they will be preparing for a make-believe press conference. Briefly explain to students the purpose of a press conference.

2. Instruct students to prepare between five and ten talking points about the concept or topic that has been presented in the lesson. It may help to show students a brief example of a press conference. Talking points are typically the most important parts of the message that a person wants to ensure that everyone understands.

3. Provide students with time to review their notes, materials, books, and other resources.

4. If appropriate, ask students to review with partners or do an **Add On** activity or a **Team Web**.

5. Provide students with time to write, edit, and review their talking points.

6. Collect the talking points and if time permits, have students hold mock press conferences in small groups or as a whole class.

■ Tips and Variations

♦ The talking points could be collected as a **Ticket Out The Door**.

♦ The talking points could be used as part of an introduction to a follow-up lesson or as a review to prepare for an assessment.

♦ **Critical Thinking Connection**—Just as in real life, the talking points could be shared, edited, and proofed with the help of peers before conducting a press conference.

Quick Write

■ Overview

Quick Write is a versatile strategy that offers students a chance to reflect on the key points and objectives of the lesson. In addition to helping students summarize their thoughts, it can serve as a quick and easy assessment tool for the teacher.

■ Step by Step

1. Provide each student with a piece of paper, a 3x5 card, an **Individual Student Whiteboard**, a Post-It Note, or a journal.

2. Give students a prompt, question, or topic and explain how it is related to the objectives of the lesson.

3. Instruct students to write a short statement about the concept being learned. The statement should be brief and summarize a main point or something they understand about the topic.

4. Once students have completed the **Quick Write**, the statements can be used during partner discussions, collected as a **Ticket Out The Door**, or combined by groups to use with a **Partner Pretest**.

5. As the lesson ends, collect the **Quick Write** responses.

■ Tips and Variations

♦ Consider combining **Quick Write** with a **Team Web** or a **Snowball Fight**.

♦ Depending on student ability levels, a **Quick Write** can include key words, single sentences, lists of characteristics, or examples.

♦ Older students can do a **Quick Write** in a section of their notes or notebooks.

♦ Consider starting a subsequent lesson by handing back the **Quick Write** as a **Ticket In the Door**.

6 Words or Less

■ Overview

For many students, it is more difficult to be precise than wordy when describing key learning or understanding of a topic. With this strategy, students are asked to make a statement/write a sentence about the concept or topic being studied. The statement they create must be a complete thought in a sentence of six words or less.

■ Step by Step

1. Provide each student with a piece of paper, a 3x5 card, a Post-It Note, an **Individual Student Whiteboard**, or a journal.

2. Instruct students to think about the main ideas presented in the lesson. If appropriate, ask them to summarize their thoughts with a partner.

3. After students have had time to consider their ideas and thoughts about the content, tell them that they will be writing one sentence that communicates their thoughts and learning.

4. Tell students that the sentence should be fewer than seven words but should still communicate a clear idea about what they've learned. The statement should be a complete thought but not necessarily follow all grammar and punctuation rules.

5. Encourage students to first write out their ideas/thoughts as a draft and then replace or delete works until they get to **6 Words or Less**.

6. Example—For students learning multiplication concepts:

    Multiplication = Easier than adding by hand!

■ Tips and Variations

♦ Consider combing **6 Words or Less** with a **Ticket Out the Door, Send-A-Problem**, or **2 Truths and a Lie**.

♦ Some students may benefit from the use of a **Sentence Starter** to prompt their thinking.

♦ **6 Words or Less** could be done first as a solo/independent activity and then shared in small groups or with the whole class.

♦ **Critical Thinking Connection**—This strategy could be easily differentiated by asking some students to list six synonyms or antonyms, six examples of the topic, or six key words associated with the concept.

Sneak Peek

■ Overview

We all appreciate a good "heads up" or advanced notice of what information, activities, and plans that will be coming in the future. This strategy provides students with a preview of the next lesson and helps to show how it relates to the current concept.

■ Step by Step

1. Tell students that you'd like to give them a preview of something important. As an analogy, briefly explain to students why movie theatres provide previews of upcoming movies. (To produce interest, excitement, and to get people to talk about the movie.)

2. Tell students what they'll be learning during the next lesson. Provide examples, **Fantastic Facts**, **Quotes**, or **Stories** to gain student interest.

3. Ask students to make connections between the **Sneak Peek** they were just given and the content they already know.

4. Example—"Students, tomorrow we are going to begin a unit on geography. Now geography is not just the study of mountains, streams, and oceans. Did you know that the man who is considered the best basketball player of all time majored in geography in college? Yes, Michael Jordan majored in cultural geography at the University of North Carolina. Tomorrow I'll tell you exactly what cultural geography is and I'll even share some quotes about it directly from Jordan."

■ Tips and Variations

♦ Consider using images or pictures in the **Sneak Peek** to heighten student interest.

♦ To be effective, the **Sneak Peek** only needs to last a few minutes and could be combined with **Sentence Starters**, **Word Splash**, a **Ball Toss**, or **Keepers and Wishers**.

Ticket Out the Door

■ Overview

Teachers appreciate this strategy because it provides for student accountability at the end of a lesson. Students are instructed that the teacher will stand at the door at the end of the period (or during a time of transition) and will collect each student's **Ticket Out the Door**.

■ Step by Step

1. Provide each student with a 3x5 card, Post-It Note, or small piece of paper.

2. Give students an overview of the key points of the lesson and provide them with time to think about what they have learned and will remember most.

3. Tell students to briefly write down what they learned. For example, have students write down three dots/bullets and then list three things that they recall, learned, remembered, or thought about the topic.

4. While students leave the room, stand at the door and collect a card from each student.

5. Use the information on the tickets to gauge understanding or the progress of individual students. This information is helpful in considering what information may need to be re-taught.

■ Tips and Variations

♦ The **Circle, Triangle, Square** strategy is a popular **Ticket Out the Door** option.

♦ Remember to provide students enough time during the end of the lesson to think and reflect. If students are asked to do a **Ticket Out the Door** in the last 20 seconds before a transition, they'll likely worry more about being late for the next class and won't take the time to thoughtfully reflect.

♦ Some students may benefit from the use of **Sentence Starters** in combination with the **Ticket Out the Door**.

♦ The tickets can be used to help begin the next day's lesson or they can be used as a discussion starter with individual students.

What Did You Hear?

■ Overview

Regardless of the content we teach, what a student *hears* (in this case what they understand or think they understand) is the most important feature in assessing their understanding of the content. It is important for teachers to take the time to compare what students heard/understood verses what they wanted them to hear or understand. This strategy offers teachers the chance to assess what students heard.

■ Step by Step

1. Provide students with time to think about the main ideas and concepts presented during the lesson. If necessary, review key terms or ideas from the lesson.

2. When cued, instruct students that they will either write or discuss with partners *what they heard the teacher say* during the lesson. Encourage students to recall actual quotes, words, or phrases used by the teacher.

3. If appropriate, provide students with a **Sentence Starter** such as:

    "I heard the teacher say _____."

    "The most important thing I heard the teacher say was _____."

4. Have students discuss with partners or conduct a **Quick Write**.

■ Tips and Variations

◆ Consider combing this activity with a **Journal Response**, a **Pass It**, or **Add On**.

◆ If students struggle to recall actual quotes or phrases, tell them to use their own words to summarize what was heard.

◆ Be sure not to embarrass students or make them feel badly if they are unable to recall what was said. As an informal assessment strategy, the goal should be to accurately gauge what students have understood. If students are unable to communicate what they know, consider it an opportunity to re-teach.

◆ **Critical Thinking Connection**—Place students in pairs or small groups and ask them to critique, challenge, or confirm the statements of their partners.

Word Splash

■ **Overview**

This strategy offers students a fun alternative to discover the words, associations, and ideas that come to mind when students are prompted to think of the objective or focus of the lesson.

■ **Step by Step**

1. Provide each student with a 3x5 card, a Post-It Note, or a piece of paper.

2. Ask students to put aside all their notes, books, manipulatives, and any learning materials that are related to the content being learned.

3. Tell students that when they are cued they will write down (splash down) single words or short ideas that come to mind when given a topic.

4. Prompt students with such phrases such as, "Splash down words associated with the Scientific Method." Since the goal is to discover what immediately comes to mind, it is not necessary for students to elaborate or provide definitions.

5. Example—After learning about the Legislative Branch of government, ask students to **Word Splash** terms associated with Checks and Balances.

6. Collect the **Word Slash** cards as a **Ticket Out the Door**.

■ **Tips and Variations**

♦ An option is to ask students to divide a sheet of paper into four sections and use each section to **Word Splash** four different ideas/concepts.

♦ The ideas that are "splashed" could be color coded with highlighters according to topics or categories. For example, the color green could represent all the ideas that come to a student's mind that are easily understood. The color yellow could be used for words that are familiar but not totally comprehended and the red could be used for ideas or terms that are not fully understood.

♦ Consider using the **Word Splash** cards as part of a beginning activity in a subsequent lesson.

Part Three

Strategies for Solo/Independent Work

Content Nameplate

■ Overview

This strategy encourages students to use some creativity in the creation of a nameplate that contains important information about topics, content, people, or events being studied.

■ Step by Step

1. Provide each student with an 8.5x11 sheet of paper.

2. Instruct students to fold the paper, tent-style, so the paper can stand on its own.

3. Provide students with a list of key concepts, ideas, or terms that go along with the objectives of the lesson.

4. Lead each student to select one of the terms or randomly assign them to students.

5. Instruct students that the term, idea, or concept will be written in large letters in the middle of the **Content Nameplate** on section that will be shown when it is folded.

6. Tell students to fill each of the four corners of the nameplate with examples, content, illustrations, or definitions that relate to the term in the center of the nameplate.

7. Example—For students studying the Electoral College:

538 Electors	Based on a State's population
Electoral College	
Purpose: to elect the President & VP	Takes place once every four years

■ Tips and Variations

♦ Consider combining **Content Nameplates** with a **Gallery Walk, Send-A-Spy,** or **Timer Tell**.

♦ Provide students with a sample **Content Nameplate** as a model.

♦ **Critical Thinking Connection**—Ask students to select the information from one of the corners of the nameplate in order to elaborate on it. Have students gather additional information and create an illustration, model, story, or example.

Checklists

■ Overview

Checklists serve as a road map to help students determine which tasks and assignments needs to be accomplished. Some students are also motivated by the ability to track their accomplishments and check off items as they are completed.

■ Step by Step

1. Provide students with a blank **Checklist** form (see Checklist on page 125).

2. Review with students the tasks, assignments, or work that needs to completed and provide a specific time frame for each task.

3. Guide students to list, copy, or brainstorm the tasks that they personally need to complete in order to meet the expectations of the assignment. If appropriate, lead them to prioritize tasks according to various criteria such as:

   Easiest to complete

   Will take the most time

   Already started

   Need help getting started

   Need help finishing

4. While students are working on their tasks, periodically ask them to reflect and update their checklist.

5. Provide students with time to update their **Checklists** and celebrate their accomplishments.

■ Tips and Variations

- ♦ Consider guiding students to place the easiest task or learning at the beginning of the list. This could help build momentum and motivation.

- ♦ **Checklists** can also be used as an effective tool to communicate with home. In addition to listing and tracking tasks and accomplishments, a section can be included for parents to sign and return.

- ♦ Some students benefit from the use of multiple **Checklists** for organizing different types of tasks. These can be color coded according to the type of task.

- ♦ Consider combining **Checklists** with **Partner Pretest** or **Line Ups**.

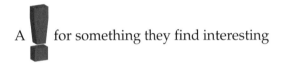

Coded Reading

■ Overview

Students typically do well when they are given a clear purpose and reason for reading. This strategy offers students a reason for reading and offers many the motivational push needed to accomplish a reading task.

■ Step by Step

1. Prior to reading a passage (particularly non-fiction) provide students with codes to use/record while reading.

2. Model for students how the codes are used including how many they should use and how often.

3. Codes could include:

A for something they find interesting

A for something they have a question about

A for something they'd like to talk about

4. As students read, ask them to highlight, record, and note the reading utilizing the assigned codes.

5. After a designated period of reading time, ask students to stop and review their codes.

6. Ask students to share one or more of their codes with partners or group students according to the types of codes they used most often.

■ Tips and Variations

♦ See **Coded Reading** on page 126 for more examples of codes to use while reading.

♦ Consider using this strategy in conjunction with **Outcome Statements, Corners,** or **Move and Touch**.

♦ **Critical Thinking Connection**—This strategy could also be used with proofing or critiquing another student's writing. In that case, be sure to provide frameworks and specific ways for students to give the feedback.

Color Code

■ Overview

The use of different colors can provide students with a clear way to organize their learning and can assist in memory, recall, and processing. Color-coded materials also help students when it comes to locating and organizing materials such as folders, handouts, and written work.

■ Step by Step

1. Provide students with different colored markers, pens, or highlighters.

2. Hand out learning materials, notes, worksheets or other items that students will use when completing learning tasks.

3. Give students a method for organizing their materials using colors.

4. Example—As students are organizing their materials and notes about the American Revolution, instruct them to highlight *events* in the color green, *personalities* in the color yellow, and *facts* in blue.

5. Provide students with time to re-organize or update their **Color Codes** or consult with their peers to compare notes.

■ Tips and Variations

♦ When students are using books that cannot be written in, provide them with different colored Post-It Notes to organize their learning.

♦ **Color Codes** work well when students are working on long-term, project-oriented tasks. In this case, have students use the **Color Codes** to organize the process of the tasks such as items to be completed by a certain date in the color red, items that can wait until the end in green, and items that need to be double checked in yellow.

♦ **Color Codes** work well in conjunction with **Checklists**.

Concept Collage

■ Overview

This strategy allows for students to be creative in the description and elaboration of their content knowledge. Although it takes a bit more preparation and oversight than some of the other strategies, the level of engagement and the ability of students to demonstrate depth of understanding is worth the extra time.

■ Step by Step

1. Provide students with resources, notes, readings, and other materials related to the concepts being learned.

2. Give students a supply of crayons, markers, glue, tape, and pictures that will help them to create a **Concept Collage.**

3. Help students to reflect on their learning by brainstorming or reviewing key ideas. Students may also need suggestions about how to organize their materials.

4. If needed, provide students with time to work with partners to review the content prior to beginning their **Concept Collage.**

5. Instruct students to find or create pictures that relate to the concepts, key ideas, or vocabulary terms that have been learned.

6. Provide time for students to create the **Concept Collages.**

■ Tips and Variations

◆ Follow up by asking students to elaborate on their **Concept Collage** with a **Journal Response,** a **Team Web,** or **Add On.**

◆ Some teachers are concerned about students who spend too much time finding and cutting pictures and not enough time relating those pictures to the content. In those cases, divide up the work time into discreet, short time blocks where students first find and cut out pictures followed by arranging and gluing followed by writing, describing or editing.

◆ Collages do not need to be complex in order to be effective. The power of **Concept Collages** lie in the fact that they are personalized and that students are asked to elaborate and explain their thoughts.

Create the Test

Overview

Students often do well when they are given the opportunity to have a direct say in how they will be evaluated. This strategy offers students the chance to create test or quiz items that will in turn be used in an assessment.

Step by Step

1. Provide students with an opportunity to review key ideas, terms, and examples from the lesson or unit. If appropriate, provide them with a chance to debrief with partners or small groups.

2. Tell students that they will have the chance to provide input, ideas, and actual questions that will be used on the next test or quiz.

3. Ask students to assemble and collect resource materials such as textbooks, notes, handouts, and worksheets related to the topic. Depending on the needs of the students, provide time for them to organize the materials in order to determine what is needed and what is not.

4. Once students have organized their materials, state how much time they'll have to work on creating the test questions and give them several examples of both good and bad test questions.

5. Give students time to work on creating the test questions. Ensure that students understand how many possible test items they are required to create. Remind them that answers or examples must be provided for each question written.

Tips and Variations

♦ Avoid giving public credit or accolades to students who create test items that are used in actual assessments. For example, don't say "Brent wrote item #3 on the test so he should at least get that one right." This could embarrass the student in addition to possibly making him a target if other students struggle with the question.

♦ Consider combining **Create the Test** with a **Mind Map**, **Team Web**, or **Add On**.

♦ This activity also serves as an informal assessment because most students will write test questions for content that is easy to understand or that has clear examples. In this case, reviewing the test questions offers the teacher the chance to see what students think is easy as well as what topics or content students *avoided* writing test questions about.

Flash Cards 2.0

Overview

Flash Cards have been used as an instructional strategy for decades. **Flash Cards 2.0** incorporates a more interactive approach and encourages students to use them in a more creative, fun way. Since students take an active part in creating, updating, and sharing the flashcards, they tend to take more ownership in them and use them for a longer period of time.

Step by Step

1. Provide students with blank 3x5 cards and markers, crayons, stickers, or other materials that will help them to customize their cards.

2. Remind students of the content being studied and, if necessary, provide them with a list of key vocabulary terms, examples, math facts, or other commercially produced cards they could copy.

3. Show students examples of customized flash cards and remind them that although they can be colorful and creative, the main goal is to ensure that the content is placed on the cards.

4. Give students time to create their cards. Ensure that they know exactly how many cards they are required to produce as well as how much time they have.

Tips and Variations

♦ Regardless of the size of the flash cards, consider hole punching them and placing them on a metal ring. Many student desks have metal or wire racks where students can place the rings.

♦ Just like traditional flash cards, the power of **Flash Cards 2.0** is in the use of them. Encourage students to review the cards during times when they have finished other work.

♦ It is important to provide students with samples and examples of customized flash cards so they have an example that shows how complex, colorful, and creative they should be.

♦ Consider combining **Flash Cards 2.0** with an **I Learned Chain**, **20 Questions**, or **Guess the Word**.

Mind Maps

Overview

This strategy has been made popular by Nancy Margulies, author of *Mapping Inner Space* as well as numerous Internet websites. It offers students the opportunity to create visual representations (maps) of their learning and it helps them to discover how content and ideas are connected.

Step by Step

1. Provide each student a piece of paper along with pens, markers, crayons, colored pencils, etc.

2. Instruct them to write the topic of study in the center of the page.

3. Guide students to brainstorm what they know about the topic and "map out" connections between topics and ideas. Encourage the use of colors, symbols, lines, arrows, icons, and diagrams in addition to text.

4. Provide additional feedback, resources, texts, or other materials that will assist students in creating their mind maps.

5. Give students time to work on creating their **Mind Maps**.

Tips and Variations

♦ Many students will start with a traditional spider diagram until they see connections between topics. The teacher may have to help students make direct connections between ideas, concepts, or terms.

♦ Remind students that each of the **Mind Maps** will look very different from each other.

♦ Students often take a lot of pride in their maps because they represent effort, creativity, and personal connections.

♦ Provide time for students to periodically revisit their **Mind Maps** in order to expand ideas and discover additional connections.

♦ Consider combining **Mind Maps** with a **Partner Protest**, a **Gallery Walk**, **Send-A-Spy**, or a **Quick Write**.

♦ **Critical Thinking Connection**—Ask students to select a certain section of their **Mind Map** in order to explain and elaborate upon the ideas presented. Consider using a **Sentence Starter** such as, "If you were to explain this concept to a group of younger students, what would you say?"

MIP

■ Overview

Teachers sometimes struggle to get students to understand the most important parts of an objective or lesson. This strategy asks students to think about the **Most Important Point**, idea, example, or piece of information from a lesson, text, or assignment.

■ Step by Step

1. Provide students with time to work independently on an academic task.

2. Instruct students that while they are working on their assignment, you will ask them to pause at various points in order to consider the most important point of what they are currently reading, writing, or doing.

3. If the **MIP**s will be collected rather than written in a notebook or on a worksheet, provide students with guidance about the form of the **MIP** (complete sentences, a picture summary, etc).

4. Get student attention and prompt them to think about what they were working on before being interrupted.

5. Ask students to write down what they consider to be the **MIP** of what they were learning.

6. Example—"Students, please look up here. I have an important task for you. Think about what you were just reading about volcanoes. Most of you were reading pages 17 to 21 of the science textbook. Think for a moment about the most important thing you read about in that section. Please write your **MIP** on a Post-It Note. When you have written your **MIP**, you may proceed with the reading."

■ Tips and Variations

♦ Consider combining **MIP** with **My Top 10 List**, an **I Learned Chain**, or a **Give One/ Get One**.

♦ An option is to have students to write the **MIP** on a piece of paper and collect all the papers for use in a review, as a strategy to begin a lesson, in a discussion, or as preparation for an assessment.

♦ When reading a book, provide students with Post-It Notes and ask them to write their MIP on the note and place it in the book next to where that information or example was found.

My Top 10 List

■ Overview

This strategy is powerful because it helps students to become aware of the key points of the learning and can provide insight into what information still needs to be learned.

■ Step by Step

1. Provide students with a pre-printed **My Top 10 List** (see My Top 10 List on page 127) or ask them to take out a sheet of paper and list the numbers 1 to 10 or ten bullet points.

2. Instruct students that while they are working independently, they will be asked to list ten important things they are learning. Those ten items could include examples, definitions, terms, or illustrations.

3. During student work time, pause at regular intervals and prompt students to add important ideas and concepts to their list.

4. In some cases, it may be appropriate to prompt students to write specific items on their list.

5. Instruct students that their top ten items will likely be expanded and revised as they learn more about a topic.

■ Tips and Variations

♦ Depending on the instructional level of the students, they could either summarize in their own words or copy information directly from a source.

♦ The top ten ideas, examples, or terms complied by students offers the teacher a glimpse into what information seems most important to them and what may need to be covered in more depth. For example, "Students, when I was reviewing your top ten lists I noticed that only a few of you listed the concept of Imperialism as being in your top ten. Please add that because it is a very important concept."

♦ Consider combining **My Top 10 List** with **Partner Pretest**, **Create the Test**, or as a reference in **Consultation**.

♦ **Critical Thinking Connection**—Provide time for students to review their lists and ask them to select between one to three items for additional elaboration. When those additional items have been selected, lead students to identify or create connections between the ideas.

Picture This

■ Overview

A visual representation of a concept can serve as a powerful tool to help students deepen their understanding. This strategy calls for students to create a picture to represent relationships among topics.

■ Step by Step

1. Provide students with a blank sheet of paper, a 3x5 card, or a Post-It Note.

2. Prompt students to think about the main ideas, concepts, or details of the current assignment they are completing. Ask students to choose several concepts, details, or ideas from their learning. If necessary, provide students with a listing of key ideas, terms, or examples.

3. Instruct students to create a picture summary for each of the concepts specifically focusing on how the various concepts relate to each other. Ask students to create the picture using as few words as possible.

4. Provide students with models and samples of acceptable **Picture This** products. Once the visuals are completed, ask students to create a **6 Words or Less** summary and affix the visuals to notes or worksheets.

■ Tips and Variations

♦ **Picture This** differs from a **Quick Draw** in that it is typically more elaborate and asks students to make connections between several related concepts as opposed to one discrete idea or fact.

♦ Some students may benefit from guidance about how to choose the ideas for their picture as well as how to begin their picture. For example, they could be asked to create a picture for the most complicated concept, the concept with the most examples, or the concept that will most likely appear on an assessment.

♦ Students could tape or staple their **Picture This** products into their notes or the teacher could collect them and use them in preparation for an assessment or as a **Ticket In the Door**.

♦ The **Picture This** products could be collected, hole punched, placed on a metal ring and used in conjunction with a **Partner Pretest**.

♦ **Critical Thinking Connection**—Provide students with pictures of different items and ask student to do a **Forced Analogy** or draw their own version of that object in order to represent the concept.

RSS Feed

■ Overview

RSS stands for Really Simple Syndication and is a method used by websites to provide updates to subscribers and users of their sites. **RSS Feeds** typically provide subscribers only with updates of newly posted information. This strategy uses that concept to ask students to *update* their knowledge on a topic.

■ Step by Step

1. Briefly instruct students on the definition and purpose of an **RSS Feed**. If appropriate, provide an example of a website that uses an **RSS Feed**. Point out that **RSS Feeds** are updates and allow the reader to see what is new or recently updated.

2. Provide students with time to study, read, or discover information, examples, or details about the content being studied. Ask them to focus on what they are learning that is new. If necessary, allow them the opportunity to share with a partner.

3. Provide students with a half sheet of paper or ask them to find a space in their notes.

4. Instruct them to write an **RSS Feed** for one specific topic where they have learned new or updated information. In most cases, students have learned several new things. In that case, either ask them to focus on one idea or provide them with time to create several **RSS Feeds**.

5. Have students place the **RSS Feed** in their notes or collect them to use with a subsequent activity or a partner discussion.

■ Tips and Variations

♦ **RSS Feeds** typically consist of a few lines describing the update and, if needed, a link to the full story or content.

♦ There are several websites that provide **RSS Feed** readers including Google. In addition, many educationally related websites offer **RSS Feeds** to their readers.

♦ **Critical Thinking Connection**—For students that struggle to find (or admit) anything new, ask them to elaborate on a concept that they already know well or ask them to create an **RSS Feed** for a specific audience. For example, ask them to create an **RSS Feed** of the content for a younger student.

2 Truths and a Lie

■ Overview

Just like the popular ice-breaker game, this strategy asks students to create three statements about the content they are learning. Two of the statements need to be true while the third should be a lie but stated in such a way that it would be believable and cause the reader to pause and think about their answer.

■ Step by Step

1. Provide each student with a 3x5 card.

2. Ask them to consider the content being learned and provide think time and, if appropriate, time to share with a partner.

3. Instruct students that they are going to create three statements about the content being learned. Two of the statements will be true but unique enough to make someone think twice about it. One statement will be false but also unique enough to make the students pause and think.

4. Provide students with time to think, research, and write their statements.

5. Ask students to share these statements with partners or collect the cards as a **Ticket Out the Door**.

6. Example—For students studying the Legislative Branch of the Federal Government:

    The Legislative Branch creates laws. (true)

    The Vice President serves as President of the Senate. (true)

    The Legislative Branch is made up of the Senate, the House of Representatives, and members of the President's Cabinet. (lie)

■ Tips and Variations

♦ This strategy can be easily differentiated by asking students of different abilities to create statements of varying complexity or detail.

♦ As an option, on the back of the 3x5 cards, students could be asked to list book page numbers or a brief citation showing where they got the information that created the statements.

♦ Consider combining **2 Truths and a Lie** with a **Ball Toss**, **Inside/Outside Circle**, or **Stump the Teacher**.

Txt Message

Overview

Technology is an integral part of our daily lives and many of our students are expert "texters." This strategy uses their knowledge of texting as a novel way for them to "send" text messages to their peers.

Step by Step

1. Provide students with a **Txt Message** template (see Txt Message on page 128) or provide them with a 3x5 card or a half sheet of paper.

2. Inform students that they will be creating text messages related to the content they are learning. Provide them with a few examples of content-related text messages.

3. Remind students that text messages are typically short in nature and do not have to contain proper grammar or complete sentences. The purpose of the text message is to communicate important content they have learned.

4. During independent learning time, prompt the students to stop and think about what they were currently learning. Then ask them to write a brief **Txt Message** describing an idea, concept, or example.

5. The **Txt Messages** can be collected by the teacher, used with a partner or small group discussion, or collected as a **Ticket Out the Door**.

Tips and Variations

♦ Some teachers may be reluctant to try this strategy because some students will ask if they can use their real cell phones for this activity. Each teacher should consult with their principal to determine the correct way to address this question.

♦ Some students can be creative in the use of symbols, emoticons, and letters to create inappropriate messages. Teachers should be savvy and up to date on the meanings

♦ Some teachers are concerned that using "texting" language diminishes student writing ability. The purpose of this activity is for students to communicate their knowledge of the *content* being studied. As a result, the writing ability does not necessarily need to be evaluated.

Part Four

Strategies for the Whole Group

Choral Response

■ Overview

Choral responses are a staple in classrooms with active learning. Although typically associated with primary grade levels, **Choral Responses** can be a valuable tool with all age groups.

■ Step by Step

1. Prior to a lesson, determine key words, concepts, definitions, or facts that students need to recall.

2. During the lesson, pause and tell students that they will be asked to repeat aloud various important words, ideas, or facts.

3. Either on the board or on a sheet of paper, provide students with a listing of the ideas or words to be repeated.

4. Instruct students in the method they should use when chorally responding to teacher prompts. This should include the prompt that will be used to cue them to respond as well as the way they should respond.

5. Pause during the lesson and lead students to chorally respond to questions or prompts.

6. Example—For students studying terms related to fractions:

   "Students, in just a moment when I say the words *your turn*, I want you all to say aloud the term that we use to describe the top number in a fraction."

■ Tips and Variations

♦ For older students, ask them to chorally respond regarding assignment details such as due dates or essential components to be included in a task.

♦ For a fun twist, ask students to chorally respond using different voices such as a whisper, a growl, or with an accent.

♦ Some teachers prefer to use the "My turn, our turn, your turn" method when having students chorally respond.

♦ Consider combining a **Choral Response** with **20 Questions** or **Outcome Statements**.

Common Songs

■ Overview

Teachers can tap into the power of music, melody, and rhythm by incorporating familiar songs into their lessons by using the melodies of common songs with lyrics that reflect the content being learned.

■ Step by Step

1. Give students a listing of important concepts key vocabulary words, or an outline of the content.

2. Provide students with an opportunity to summarize what they have learned so far in the lesson using a **Halftime Summary** or **6 Words or less.**

3. Instruct students that they will be using the melodies to common song(s) as a way to help them remember important content.

4. Provide an example of songs that can be used and ask for volunteers to sing the melodies.

5. Lead students to select a common song.

6. Give students time to create lyrics, using the content being studied, that go along with the song they selected.

7. If appropriate, ask students to share their songs and lyrics with partners or the whole group.

■ Tips and Variations

♦ See **Common Songs** on page 129 for a larger listing of common songs with simple melodies.

♦ Many teachers prefer to use the whole group setting to present the idea of using common songs and then placing students in smaller groups to collaborate on the lyrics and create and practice the song.

♦ Some teachers struggle with the idea of allowing students to create lyrics to current, popular songs. Sticking with older, more commonly accepted children's songs are the best bet. Some students will groan that they can't use hip-hop, rap, or current rock songs, but the focus should stay on learning the content, not on selecting and using a "cool" song.

♦ Popular and easy to remember songs include: This Old Man, Twinkle, Twinkle Little Star, the Theme to the Adams Family, Jingle Bells, Old MacDonald, La Cucaracha, and the Theme to the Brady Bunch.

Fish Bowl

Overview

Just like fish in a bowl, this strategy allows students to see, hear, and observe what other students think about a concept, question, or scenario.

Step by Step

1. If possible, arrange the seating in the room in a circle or half-circle.

2. As an analogy, tell students that fish in a bowl live in an environment where everyone can see what they are doing. When we watch fish in a bowl, we observe how they live. Although we can't see what fish think, we can observe how they act.

3. Place two or three students in chairs in the center of the group and give them a topic or question to discuss. Consider having students use a **Sentence Starter** to begin the conversation. Tell students that they will have a discussion for approximately 2 minutes.

4. When cued, the students in the **Fish Bowl** start to have a discussion centered on the topic or prompt provided by the teacher. Students can provide answers, give examples, or state opinions.

5. The students on the outside are instructed to follow along with the conversation because they may be asked to join the conversation at any given time.

6. When appropriate, the teacher asks the students in the **Fish Bowl** to pause and then selects a student to enter the **Fish Bowl** and replace one of the members.

7. The newest member of the **Fish Bowl** then continues the discussion.

8. The teacher changes questions, asks for clarification, or provides additional **Sentence Starters**.

Tips and Variations

♦ When in the **Fish Bowl**, some students may benefit from being given a specific order for the discussion and how long they should explain their opinion.

♦ If reluctant or shy students will be asked to join the **Fish Bowl**, prompt them with **Planted Questions** in order to provide them with time to consider their answer.

♦ Consider combing a **Fish Bowl** with **Envelope Questions**, **Outcome Statements**, **MIP**, or **My Top 10 List**.

Forced Analogies

■ Overview

Analogies are a natural part of communication and students use comparative language every day. **Forced Analogies** offer students the opportunity to think about the content or ideas in a way that compares two unlike ideas or terms.

■ Step by Step

1. Ask students to think about and reflect on what they know or have learned about the topic being studied.

2. Provide students with a brief definition of analogies including examples and characteristics.

3. On the board, overhead, or on handouts, provide students with sample analogies to choose from and ask them to relate the analogies directly to the content being learned.

4. Ask students to share their analogies with partners or complete a **Quick Write**.

5. Examples of **Forced Analogies** include:

    "_____ is like a brick wall because…"

    "How can _____ be like a pair of glasses?"

    "How is _____ similar to a bowl of cereal?"

■ Tips and Variations

♦ Humorous or novel analogies serve the dual purpose of incorporating fun and laughter and helping students to retain information.

♦ See Forced Analogies on page 130 for a list of additional **Forced Analogies**.

♦ Consider combining this strategy with **Give One/Get One** or use as a **Journal Response**.

♦ **Critical Thinking Connection**—Challenge students create their own Forced Analogies. Encourage students to share these analogies, and possible responses, with other students.

Guess the Word

■ Overview

This is a questioning strategy that challenges students to consider definitions and characteristics of key words or ideas being studied.

■ Step by Step

1. Provide students with a list of terms, vocabulary words, or concepts that are part of a lesson or unit of study.

2. Instruct students that they will be given clues about some of the ideas that are being studied and that their job is to think about the answer. When cued they will provide a response.

3. Begin by making statements about a term and ask the students to guess which word is being described. Remember to provide students with think time to consider their responses. If appropriate, ask students to consult with a partner to compare answers.

4. When cued, ask students to write their answer on a sheet of paper or on **Individual Student Whiteboards**.

5. Example—For students studying geometry terms:

   "I am thinking of a word that defines when two lines meet and share a common point." (intersection)

   "This word is used to describe one specific location. It is often labeled with a number or a letter." (point)

   "When you have a line that is closed at one end and open at the other, what is it called?" (ray)

■ Tips and Variations

♦ Ask student to create **Guess the Word** prompts or questions after they have learned the content.

♦ Consider combining Guess the Word with **Create the Test,** a **Mind Map**, or a **Choral Response**.

♦ **Critical Thinking Connection**—Challenge student to use synonyms, antonyms, or characteristics for the clues instead of just definitions.

I Learned Chain

■ Overview

This strategy offers students a visual, concrete representation of the depth and breadth of learning taking place during a unit of study. Students use strips of paper to create a large chain that includes details or facts demonstrating what they have learned. The links eventually form a long chain that can be used to illustrate the students' knowledge of a topic.

■ Step by Step

1. Provide each student with between one and five strips of paper approximately 8 inches long by 2 inches wide. (Measurements do not need to be exact.)

2. Instruct students to select key ideas, examples, or pieces of information from the content being studied. If necessary, provide guidance about the type of information to be selected.

3. Provide students with 3 to 5 minutes to review their notes or resources in order to choose those facts, definitions, details, or examples that seem important.

4. Instruct students write one key piece of information on *each* strip of paper. If a student has identified three ideas, they use three strips of paper; a separate idea is placed on each strip.

5. Once students have completed writing ideas, they link the strips together using a stapler or tape. Lead students to loop the strips together like the links in a chain.

6. Lead groups of students to link their chains together, eventually assembling one large chain. Display the chain for students or use it as a tool for a partner discussion.

■ Tips and Variations

♦ Instead of connecting the links to form a long chain, students could connect the links end to end to form one long strip of paper.

♦ Depending on the speed at which students link their chains together, the teacher could collect all the strips of paper and link them for students or have one classroom helper or aide link them together.

♦ **I Learned Chains** can be combined with **Color Codes** in a way that different colored strips can represent different types of content. Some teachers ask students to complete links during a centers activity that takes place over several days.

♦ As students develop deeper ideas or create more examples, additional links can be added to the chain.

Individual Student Whiteboards

■ Overview

This strategy, a student favorite, combines the novelty of whiteboards with an interactive element that also serves as an easy assessment tool for the teacher.

■ Step by Step

1. Provide each student with a white board, marker, and eraser.

2. Pose a question or problem to the students and provide time for them to consider their answer. If necessary, allow students to consult with a partner to compare answers.

3. Ask students to write their answers on their whiteboards.

4. When cued, have the students show their answers to the teacher or to their partners.

5. After students have shown or shared their answers, have them erase their boards in preparation for another question.

■ Tips and Variations

♦ For students that don't use the whiteboards appropriately, allow them to participate using a blank sheet of paper.

♦ Instead of having students erase their boards after each question, have them use their markers to divide the board into 4 quadrants. That way, the teacher can ask four questions before the board needs to be erased.

♦ Consider combining **Individual Student Whiteboards** with **Line Ups**, **Stand When**, or **Whip Around**.

♦ In order to prevent students from copying each other's answers, some teachers prefer to ask students to hold their whiteboards at shoulder level when showing their answers.

♦ Types of responses to be written on whiteboards can include: single word responses, lists, characteristics, ideas, facts, examples, graphic representations, and agree/disagree statements.

Oh Yeah Stickers

■ Overview

Students of all ages, even if the won't admit it, enjoy receiving stickers on their papers. This strategy combines the novelty of stickers with student choice about what they most want to remember from a lesson.

■ Step by Step

1. Provide each student with a sticker or a selection of stickers.

2. Give students time to review their notes, worksheets, or other written material. If needed, provide them an opportunity to share important ideas with partners.

3. Instruct students to place a sticker next to a concept, idea, or example that they feel is important.

4. Provide students with an opportunity to discuss with partners the reason they placed the stickers where they did. ("Oh yeah, I remember why I put that sticker there.")

5. Collect student papers (the ones with the stickers on them) or ask students to hold on to them until the next day.

■ Tips and Variations

- ◆ In subsequent lessons, ask students to take out the papers that have the **Oh Yeah Stickers** on them. Provide students with time to review their notes and think about why they put the sticker next to that idea or term.

- ◆ Stickers do not need to be expensive or directly related to the content. Simple, colored dot stickers will be sufficient.

- ◆ Consider using **Oh Yeah Stickers** with a **Ticket Out the Door**, a **Quick Draw**, or a **Move and Touch**.

- ◆ The papers with the **Oh Yeah Stickers** could be collected and analyzed by the teacher to determine what the entire class or subgroups of students thought was important to remember.

- ◆ **Critical Thinking Connection**—Stickers could be categorized according to self-reflection questions prompted by the teacher. For example, star stickers could be placed next to content the students feel they know well, a red sticker could be placed next to something the students need to revisit or practice, or a "Good Job" sticker could be placed next to something students should show their parents.

On Deck Questions

- ## Overview

  Just like in the game of baseball, this strategy asks students to be the "On Deck" batters in order to prepare for participation in the lesson.

- ## Step by Step

  1. When explaining this strategy to students, it may be helpful to explain that in the game of baseball, the person waiting to bat next is often asked to warm up, swing their bat, and get ready in a location called the "On Deck" circle. The "On Deck" batter is instructed to watch the game closely in order to determine what may happen next. They are asked to play close attention to the pitcher (the teacher) in order to anticipate what type of pitch (question) will be thrown next.

  2. Explain to students that that all players (students) will need to get ready for **On Deck Questions** during the lesson.

  3. Call on students and tell them they are now batting and they need to determine *the next question, topic, or example* that they think the teacher will ask (the next pitch being thrown).

  4. Provide think time and, if necessary, an opportunity for students to consult with a partner in order to consider the next question(s).

  5. Example—The teacher calls "On Deck" and instructs the players (students) to consider the next pitch (question) in the game (lesson) by responding with, "*The next question the teacher will ask is . . .*"

- ## Tips and Variations

  - ◆ Some students may benefit from combining this strategy with **Sentence Starters** or a **Quick Write** response.

  - ◆ Since participation by all students is the goal, every student is expected to be "On Deck" and prepared to enter the "game."

  - ◆ **Critical Thinking Connection**—Note that the focus here is on determining the questions to ask, not the correct answers. Determining questions allows for deeper conversations than merely repeating back correct answers.

Response Cards

◾ Overview

Students need opportunities to participate using strategies that are low stress and non-threatening. **Response Cards** allow students the chance to participate in a way that is comfortable but also allows the teacher to assess their understanding and participation.

◾ Step by Step

1. Using scratch paper or index cards, have students create response cards such as True/False, Fact/Opinion, Yes/No, etc.

2. Pose a question to students that can be answered using the **response cards**.

3. Provide wait time and, if appropriate, ask students to consult with a partner to consider their answer.

4. When given a cue, instruct students to use their cards to indicate their response to the question.

◾ Tips and Variations

- Other examples of **Response Cards** include: A/B/C/D, Add/Subtract, ?/!/., or terms being studied during the lesson.

- For younger students, **Response Cards** in the form of animals, pictures, or icons can be used.

- See Response Cards on page 131 for reproducible **Response Cards** to use with students.

Send-A-Problem

■ Overview

Popularized by Dr. Spencer Kagan as a Cooperative Learning structure, this strategy allows individuals or groups of students to pose questions, problem, or scenarios for other students in the class.

■ Step by Step

1. Provide each student with a 3x5 card, a Post-It Note, or a half sheet of paper.

2. Give students time to review their notes, handouts, or other materials related to the content being studied. If necessary, provide students with time to have a brief partner discussion in order to review their ideas, questions, or thoughts.

3. Instruct each student to create a question, based on the content being learned, that requires an explanation. Students should avoid creating questions that can be answered with a yes/no or a one-word answer.

4. Lead students to write the question on one side of their 3x5 card or paper and the answer on the other side.

5. Once all students have written their questions and answers, collect all the cards.

6. Randomly distribute the cards to students. Instruct them to look at only one side of the card. At this point, it doesn't matter if students are reading the question or answer side of the card.

7. Depending on the side of the card students are reading, ask them to either consider an answer to the question or to create a question that goes along with the answer provided.

■ Tips and Variations

♦ Considering combining **Send-A-Problem** with a **Snowball Fight, Create the Test, or Keepers and Wishers.**

♦ For reluctant students, permit them to work in pairs to create the questions for the **Send-A-Problem** cards. Provide each student in a pair with a specific task to complete. For example, one partner could brainstorm questions while the other could find answers.

♦ As a review activity in preparation for an assessment, collect all the **Send-A-Problem** cards as a **Ticket Out the Door** at the end of a lesson. The next day, distribute the cards randomly to students as a **Ticket In the Door.**

Stump the Teacher

■ Overview

This strategy is a variation of **20 Questions** where students are challenged to create questions, hints, and lists with the purpose of trying to **Stump the Teacher**.

■ Step by Step

1. Provide students with time to review materials, handouts, and books related to the content being studied.

2. Instruct each student to write 5 to 10 questions about the content being studied. Students must provide both the question and the answer.

3. Provide students with time to research, write, and answer their questions.

4. Place students in pairs or small groups and instruct them to review all the questions written by each group member.

5. Lead the groups to select the five most difficult questions that they believe will **Stump the Teacher**.

6. Back with the whole group, call on students to ask their questions. The teacher then either guesses the term or idea or asks follow-up questions in order to get more information.

■ Tips and Variations

♦ The groups of students could arrange the questions according to different criteria such as easiest to most difficult or one word to multiword answers.

♦ Consider combing **Stump the Teacher** with the **Add On** or **Team Web** strategies.

♦ **Critical Thinking Connection**—The power of this strategy is in the creation of the questions, not in guessing the correct answer. The process of creating questions forces the students to think more deeply about the content.

Take-A-Breath

■ Overview

This is a simple, yet powerful strategy that asks students to say aloud the words, ideas, or terms that are associated with a unit of study.

■ Step by Step

1. Pause midway through the lesson and ask students to clear their mind and take a deep breath.

2. Remind students, in one sentence, of the topic and objective of the lesson.

3. Tell students that on the count of three, they will say aloud the first word that comes to mind that is related to the content. Help students to understand that the purpose is to help the teacher assess what first comes to mind when they think of a word. It may be helpful to explain that **Take-A-Breath** is a kind of association game.

4. Example—For students studying Earth Science:

   "Students, I want everyone to place their pencils, materials, and books down on their desk. Everyone take a deep breath. In just a moment, when I count to 3, I want everyone to say aloud the first word that comes to mind that is related to plate tectonics."

■ Tips and Variations

♦ Consider combining **Take-A-Breath** with a **Choral Response** in order to clarify important points.

♦ This strategy serves as both a relaxation exercise for the students but also a good informal assessment for the teacher.

♦ Other options after students **Take-A-Breath** include students whisper the one-word associations to a partner, shout the words loudly, shout but cover their mouths to muffle the noise, or write the word on an **Individual Student Whiteboard**.

♦ This strategy can be expanded upon by adding specific content after students have taken a deep breath. In the example above, add, "I want everyone to say aloud the first word that comes to mind related to *faults*."

Timer Tell

■ Overview

Students often thrive when given a specific time frame for completion of a task. The **Timer Tell** strategy relies on the use of a timer in order to help students keep focused and engaged.

■ Step by Step

1. Provide each student with a sheet of paper and a pen or a pencil.

2. Instruct students that a timer will be set and that they will be asked to write, non-stop, about a prompt until the timer goes off.

3. Set the timer for between 30 to 60 seconds and provide students with a prompt such as, *"Write about the different ways pronouns can be used in a sentence."*

4. When the timer goes off, place students in pairs or small groups.

5. Set the timer again for 30 seconds and tell students that they will tell their partners what they wrote on their papers. One student is to talk for the entire 30 seconds until the timer goes off.

6. Each partner in the group should be given the same time to share what they wrote.

■ Tips and Variations

♦ If possible, use a visual timer that can be displayed on the wall or overhead.

♦ One novel alternative is to have a student set the timer but not to tell anyone else, the teacher included, how much time will be set.

♦ Provide students with suggestions about what to do if they get stuck and can't think of anything more to say or write. For example, they could repeat what they already said, summarize someone else's ideas, or think of examples.

♦ Consider combining **Timer Tell** with **Sentence Starters, Pass It,** or **Unique Idea Only**.

♦ It is possible to have students talk for 30 seconds before writing. However, writing first provides students with specific content to discuss during **Timer Tell**.

20 Questions

■ Overview

Just like the popular game, this strategy requires students to ask questions to the teacher in an effort to figure out the concept, term, detail, or fact that the teacher is considering.

■ Step by Step

1. Provide students with an overview of the objective(s) of the lesson or unit and, if necessary, time to review any materials, handouts, or resources they have about the content.

2. Instruct students that they will be playing a game of **20 Questions** where they have to figure what words, ideas, or concepts the teacher is thinking about.

3. Remind students of the rules of the game of **20 Questions**. Each student, when called upon, will ask one question of the teacher. The question must be able to be responded to with either a "yes" or "no" answer. If the student asks a question that is answered with a "no," another student has a chance to ask a question. This process continues until a student guesses what the teacher is thinking or the class has reached **20 Questions** without correctly determining the word or idea.

4. Provide students with sample questions they could ask in order to help determine the word or term.

5. Play **20 Questions** remembering to provide feedback to students about their questions and guesses. If appropriate, respond with such statements as, "You're getting hotter."

6. Examples of student questions include:

   "Is it an idea you talked about yesterday?"

   "Have you given an example of it?"

   "Have we read about it in our textbook?"

■ Tips and Variations

♦ This strategy allows for an easy assessment of student understanding. When students struggle to define or guess a concept, consider re-teaching those concepts or ask students to create a **My Top 10 List**.

♦ Encourage reluctant or shy students to participate by tracking the questions being asked by students in the class

♦ Partners or teams of students could work together to brainstorm questions to ask.

♦ Consider providing students with **Response Cards** in order to allow them to demonstrate what they think the teacher answer will be.

Unique Idea Only

■ Overview

This strategy helps students to discover the ideas, thoughts, and examples of other students in the class. By discovering and sharing ideas, students are able to see the limitations of their own thinking and to expand upon examples from other students.

■ Step by Step

1. Remind students of the key objectives and outcomes of the lesson.

2. Ask students to brainstorm a written list of key ideas or examples that relate to the lesson. Provide students with several minutes to brainstorm ideas.

3. After students have a written list of brainstormed ideas, tell them that they will be given the chance to see what others in the class said about the topic or question. Students will be called upon, one at a time to share one item that is on their list.

4. The first student tells a term or idea that is on their list. All the other students in the class then cross that idea (or one that is very similar) off their list.

5. The next student is then called upon to share something that has not already been shared (A **Unique Idea Only**). Again, students cross off their lists the idea that was shared.

6. This continues until all students have shared a unique idea.

7. Example—When teaching students to vary word choice in their writing, ask them to brainstorm as many ways as they can think of to say the word *said*.

■ Tips and Variations

♦ For students who struggle to get started on their brainstorm list, provide suggestions ideas, or prompts to get them started.

♦ **Unique Idea Only** helps students to see both what they have in common with other students as well as what original/unique ideas they have. It is permissible to allow pairs of students to brainstorm a list together.

♦ Typically, during a solo brainstorming session, students will get stuck after a few minutes and stop writing. When that happens, don't assume that they are done. Allow wait time, encourage them to think some more, or offer suggestions such as, "Can you think of any antonyms or synonyms for that idea?"

♦ **Critical Thinking Connection**—Challenge students to consider additional ways the unique ideas could be assembled, reported, or formatted. For example, the ideas could be graphically represented, assembled into a report, or used to develop a survey.

Part Five

Strategies for Partners and Small Groups

Add On

Overview

This strategy offers students the opportunity to first brainstorm their own ideas about a topic and then to get additional ideas from other students.

Step by Step

1. Remind students of the objectives of the lesson.

2. Allow students a few minutes to review their notes, books, or materials.

3. Provide each student with a sheet of paper. Ask them to write for 30 to 60 seconds about what they know, believe, or think about the topic.

4. When students have finished writing, instruct them to place all the papers into the middle of the table.

5. Lead students to select another student's paper and read, respond, or highlight key ideas.

6. All students should have the opportunity to **Add On** to the ideas of each person in the group. When all students have added ideas to every paper, each student retrieves their original work.

7. Students then use the additional ideas from their peers to expand on their writing.

Tips and Variations

- As an alternative for reluctant students, each partner could simply write questions, single terms, examples, or words of encouragement.

- Struggling students may benefit from specific **Sentence Starters** to use when responding to the work of their peers.

- Consider combining **Add On** with **Oh Yeah Stickers**, **Team Web,** or **Journal Response.**

- **Critical Thinking Connection**—Provide students with a checklist or rubric to use when considering the **Add On** information that has been added to their original work. Challenge them to consider which statements support their purpose, which should be reworded, and which should be deleted.

Card Sort

■ Overview

This strategy offers students the chance to organize, sort, and sequence information about the content being studied. By manipulating and sorting cards, teachers are able to see how students make connections between concepts, ideas, characters, or events.

■ Step by Step

1. Give each student a stack of blank 3x5 cards.

2. Ask individual students to write down key ideas, terms, or characteristics of the content being studied. Each idea or term should be written on a separate card.

3. In pairs or small groups, have students place all the cards together in a stack.

4. Ask students to lay out all the cards, face up. If any cards are duplicates, set one card aside.

5. Prompt students with questions about the content and ask them to move, manipulate, or show the cards that best answer the questions.

6. Example—Ask students to list, one on each card, the major and minor characters in a story, several settings of the story, and several events that take place in the story. Prompt them to sort the cards according to statements such as:

    "Select the card(s) that show the primary setting of the story."

    "Select the card(s) that list the characters who play a minor role in the story."

    "Choose the card(s) of the individuals who experienced the biggest change in the story."

    "Select the card(s) that show characters that had a conflict in the story."

■ Tips and Variations

♦ Some teachers prefer to preprint all the concepts and ideas for the cards. This may be beneficial when working with students who struggle to complete tasks in a timely manner or with students who need fewer choices.

♦ Consider combining **Card Sort** with **Partner Protest, 2 Truths and a Lie, Create the Test**, or **Envelope Questions**.

Envelope Questions

■ Overview

When students are asked to share ideas with partners or small groups, there are times when interpersonal dynamics make the group ineffective. Sometimes students don't know how to share, sometimes one student dominates a discussion, and sometimes the role of each student is unclear. This strategy offers students a clear method for exchanging ideas.

■ Step by Step

1. Prior to a lesson, brainstorm and list questions that will be asked of students during the lesson. Include a variety of questions at several Bloom's levels as well as open-ended questions.

2. Write each of those questions on a 3x5 card or on a strip of paper. Place the 3x5 cards or strips in letter-sized envelopes. Each envelope could have the same questions or the questions could be differentiated based on the needs of the group or pair that will be reading them.

3. Instruct students that they will take turns pulling cards out of the envelope one at a time. After a student pulls a card or strip out of the envelope, they answer the question.

4. The student then places the card/strip to the side and the next partner takes a turn pulling a new question out of the envelope. This process continues until all the questions have been answered.

5. Once all the cards have been pulled out of the envelopes and the questions have been answered, ask students to divide the questions into two stacks. One stack indicating questions that were easy to answer and the other with questions that were difficult. If needed, students can organize the cards on a continuum from easiest to most difficult.

■ Tips and Variations

♦ Using a **Fish Bowl** or other demonstration, show students the process for pulling cards out of the envelopes. Explain what type of answer should be provided as well how long each student should explain their answer.

♦ If appropriate, allow students the chance to pass if they pull a card/question that is too difficult or allow them to trade that card/question with another student.

♦ Combine **Envelope Questions** with a **Journal Response, I Learned Chain**, or **Keepers and Wishers**.

Halftime Summary

■ Overview

Like TV commentators who discuss the first half of a sporting event, pause mid-way through a lesson and ask students to comment on the information, ideas, or content that has been presented. Just like professional commentators, students should speak to the highlights, key "plays," events, and predict a possible outcome of the "game."

■ Step by Step

1. Approximately halfway through a lesson, pause and ask the students to consider the information that has been presented so far.

2. Explain to students that they will play the role of a sports commentator who will give the highlights and key "plays" of the first half of the lesson. If needed, provide students with ideas about how to pick out the key ideas. For example, they may look through their notes, talk with a partner, or re-read key material.

3. Provide students with time to reflect and assemble their ideas. Some students may benefit from the use of a graphic organizer or other tool to assemble their thoughts.

4. Lead students to write or list the key "plays" from the first half of the lesson.

5. Ask students to share their ideas with partners or place them in groups of three to five to assemble their ideas to briefly present to the class.

■ Tips and Variations

♦ Consider combing **Halftime Summary** with **Send-A-Spy**, **Ticket Out the Door**, an **I Learned Chain**, or a **Journal Response**.

♦ **Critical Thinking Connection**—Note that commentators give both factual information about the event as well as their *opinion* about the events. Challenge students to support their opinions based on facts, details, or examples that were provided in the lesson.

Partner Pretest

■ Overview

Students understand that preparation for a test, quiz, or assessment is important but not all students have the skills, motivation, or home support to effectively prepare on their own. This strategy allows students the chance to work with a partner in order to self-assess their readiness for a test.

■ Step by Step

1. Provide pairs of students with content flash cards, a list of key words or concepts, a listing of important questions related to the content, or problems to be solved.

2. Provide each student with an **Individual Student Whiteboard**, marker, and eraser.

3. Instruct the students that pairs will take turns pulling a card from the stack and reading the question or problem aloud to their partner. One partner asks the question or states the problem and the other partner uses their whiteboard to provide the answer.

4. When the student who has written the response is ready, they show their board to their partner to check the answer.

5. The partner who asked the question is required to check the work to make sure the answer is correct.

6. Students take turns reading the question and writing answers until all the cards or questions are gone.

7. Once all the cards or questions have been addressed, ask students to organize the cards according to their level of comfort or knowledge.

■ Tips and Variations

♦ This strategy works well in combination with **Keepers and Wishers**, as a centers-based activity, with **Yup, Nope, Maybe,** or **Fish Bowl**.

♦ Ensure that each pair of students has enough questions/flashcards for each partner to get a chance to both ask the questions and write responses.

♦ This strategy will be most successful when the teacher has provided a clear model of how the partners should take turns. The teacher should also explicitly state what to do if a student doesn't know the answer (consider the *right to pass*), and what to do if they run out of questions.

♦ If both partners get stuck and cannot come to an agreement on the correct answer to a problem, ask them to set the question or problem aside and move on. Later students could **Send-A-Spy** to see how other groups answered the question.

Q and A Match

■ Overview

This strategy encourages student-to-student exchange of ideas and provides the teacher with a quick and easy method to assess student understanding.

■ Step by Step

1. Give each student a set of 3x5 cards or Post-It Notes.

2. Provide students with time to review their materials, notes, or books with the purpose of creating questions about the content.

3. Instruct students to write questions on one card or Post-It Note and the corresponding answers on another card or Post-It Note.

4. Provide students with time to research and create their questions and answers. This step is typically done by individual students but it would be permissible to allow pairs of students to create the questions and answers collaboratively.

5. Instruct pairs or small groups to collect all the cards (those with the questions as well as those with the answers) and to shuffle them.

6. On a table, desk, or floor have the students lay all the cards out with the question or answer side showing.

7. Lead students to match the question cards with the corresponding answer card. The students should work collaboratively to match all the cards. If time permits, lead students to play a concentration-type game where they place all the cards face down and turn them over to find matches.

■ Tips and Variations

♦ Students could create more answer cards than actual question cards. In this case, ask students to create matches and connections between non-obvious pairs. In those situations where there seems to be no match for a card, ask students to create an answer or question that matches the card.

♦ Consider combining **Q and A Match** with a **Send-A-Problem**, **Change of Perspective**, **Inside/Outside Circle,** or **Forced Analogies**.

♦ As an option for struggling students, allow them to create cloze statements that can be taken directly from a book or resource. For example, "The largest planet in our solar system is _____."

♦ **Critical Thinking Connection**—Challenge students to select between one and three matched cards for the purpose of generating additional questions about the topic, creating prompts or **Sentence Starters**, or rewriting the questions for a specific audience.

Quiz Show

■ Overview

Like popular television quiz shows of the 1970s and 1980s, this strategy requires pairs of students to work together to give clues and guess words associated with the content being learned.

■ Step by Step

1. Prior to the lesson, brainstorm 10 to 15 terms, concepts, or ideas that go along with the unit of study.

2. Place students in pairs and ask them to sit facing each other. One student should face the board/front of the class and another should face away.

3. Tell students that they will be playing a game. The object of the game is to get the other student to guess the word that will be displayed on the board. The student facing the board will be giving clues to the partner facing away. The job of the clue-giver is to get their partner to guess the words that will be displayed on the screen.

4. Before the game begins, tell all the students the category that will be the focus of the first round. For example, "Students, the first round of **Quiz Show** will be a listing of characters in the story A Day No Pigs Would Die by Robert Newton Peck."

5. When cued, the student facing the board attempts to get their partner to guess the words displayed on the board without using the term.

6. When the first set of terms is finished, students switch places so each is given a chance to both give clues and guess answers.

■ Tips and Variations

- ♦ Provide students with the right to pass if they get stuck and can't figure out an answer.

- ♦ While pairs of students are best, groups of three still work.

- ♦ The real power of **Quiz Show**, like the **Wear-A-Word** strategy, is not in guessing the term but in giving the clues.

- ♦ For some students, it helps to begin with a fun topic such as *types of cereal or superheroes* so students can practice the game under low stress.

- ♦ **Critical Thinking Connection**—Play the game in the same format but tell the clue-giver to only give one word clues. After each one word clue, the partner must attempt a guess. After each guess, the team either moves on to the next term or passes.

Send-A-Spy

■ Overview

This strategy encourages students to pretend to be a "spy" with the purpose of covertly obtaining ideas, details, or facts from other students or groups in the class.

■ Step by Step

1. Instruct students that one member of their group will be asked "spy" on other groups while they are working.

2. Remind students that a true spy can do their work covertly. That is, they can spy without creating a disruption.

3. It may be necessary to reassure students that, in the classroom, it is OK to be a spy at certain times and not OK to be a spy at other times. The **Send-A-Spy** strategy should only be used when prompted by the teacher.

4. Remind students that when **Send-A-Spy** is being used, groups should not try to cover up their work or prevent the spy from gathering information. They should ignore the spy and continue on in their work.

5. When cued, one of the members of the group leaves and spies on members of the other groups to get ideas, answers, or examples to bring back to their own group. Students can take turns being the spy.

6. Some students benefit from being told exactly what to spy on from the other groups. Example—"Go look at table 6. They have a unique way of organizing their information. Maybe that will give you an idea."

■ Tips and Variations

♦ This strategy often works best when groups are working on similar projects where they can exchange or expand on each other's ideas.

♦ **Send-A-Spy** gives special needs students a specific way contribute to the outcome of the group by allowing them to be the spy who seeks out examples from other groups.

♦ Consider combing **Send-A-Spy** with a **Team Web**, **Change of Perspective**, or **Postcard to a Friend**.

Sentence Starters

■ Overview

Some students struggle to put their thoughts, ideas, and opinions into words. This strategy provides students with the actual words and phrases to use when having a partner discussion.

■ Step by Step

1. Prior to the activity, prepare sentence starters on strips of paper, 3x5 cards, handouts, or on a poster displayed in the room.

   ♦ Place students in groups of two to four and provide information about the content or topic to be discussed.

   ♦ At times during the lesson, instruct students to stop and share their ideas, thoughts, or opinions using the **Sentence Starters**.

   ♦ Examples:

     "One thing that I heard that was interesting was…"

     "An example I remember is…"

     "I remember the teacher said _____ was important because…"

■ Tips and Variations

   ♦ **Sentence Starters** are supportive of the needs of English Language Learners or other students who need additional assistance in expressing their thoughts in oral language.

   ♦ Instruct students that the **Sentence Starters** are only the beginning and that they are encouraged to elaborate and explain their ideas.

   ♦ **Sentence Starters** differ from **Outcome Statements** in a couple of ways. While **Outcome Statements** are a form of **Sentence Starters**, they are typically more personal and self-reflective in nature. Students typically choose which **Outcome Statement** to utilize. **Sentence Starters** are more typically used to support partner discussions.

   ♦ See page 132 for a list of additional **Sentence Starters**.

   ♦ **Critical Thinking Connection**—Depending on the level of the students, **Sentence Starters** can be varied to include low-level, comprehension-based questions as well as higher-level evaluation and analysis questions.

Teach One, Guess It

■ Overview

This strategy offers students a fun and safe way to interact with each other and important concepts being studied in class. In addition, it provides both the teacher and the students with a quick, easy way to assess knowledge and understanding.

■ Step by Step

1. Give each student a 3x5 card or Post-It Note.

2. Provide students with a list (as a handout, on the board, or overheard) of topics, ideas, or terms related to content being learned.

3. Instruct students to select one topic or term from the list. Tell them not to let anyone else know what term they have chosen.

4. Lead students to list between three and five key ideas, examples, definitions, or characteristics about their chosen idea. Provide time for students to read, research, or determine the key ideas to be listed on their 3x5 card.

5. Place students in pairs and have them "teach" their topic to a partner. Lead students to use **Sentence Starters** such as, "I'm thinking of an idea that..."

6. Partners take turns teaching and guessing the terms and ideas on the cards.

■ Tips and Variations

♦ Combine **Teach One, Guess It** with **Give One/Get One**. Once students have new 3x5 cards, instruct them to read the information listed on the card in order to have their partners guess the idea.

♦ Encourage students to use the information listed on the cards for **Stump the Teacher, 20 Questions,** or **Create the Test**.

♦ When the activity is completed, consider collecting the cards and assembling them for use in a centers-based activity or as a **Ticket In the Door**.

Team Web

Overview

Similar to a **Mind Map**, the **Team Web** strategy incorporates visual and graphic elements to help groups of students see connections between different content and ideas.

Step by Step

1. Place students in groups of two to four and provide each group with chart paper and a collection of different colored markers.

2. Allow the groups time to review materials, brainstorm what they know or have learned about a topic or respond to review questions.

3. Advise the groups that they will be creating a group graphic organizer that will show what they know or have learned about the topic. Tell them that each member of the group will provide their own ideas plus add to the ideas of other students.

4. Instruct each student to select a different colored marker. In the center of the chart paper one student should write the topic of the **Team Web**.

5. When cued, each student in the group will simultaneously, but independently, begin one of the legs or sections of the web. Students should add words, examples, details, or illustrations. In addition, encourage students to make connections between ideas by using arrows, lines, or other images to show that ideas are related.

6. After approximately 3 to 5 minutes, instruct students to stop working on their section and to rotate the chart paper so that each student is now looking at the work of another student.

7. Lead the students to read the section in front of them and instruct them to add additional ideas to the work of their teammates. Each student uses the same color marker they started with so that their ideas and additions are easy to identify.

8. Continue to rotate the paper so that each member of the group has the opportunity to add ideas to each section.

Tips and Variations

♦ Post the **Team Webs** around the room and use as part of a **Gallery Walk**.

♦ The use of the different colored makers allows for an easy way to assess the ideas and participation of individual students. Encourage students to sign their names on the bottom of the **Team Web** in the color ink that they used.

♦ Consider combing **Team Web** with **Send-A-Spy** or **Teleprompter**.

Teleprompter

■ Overview

The politician's favorite tool, the teleprompter, can be used as a novel way to engage students in the classroom. Public speakers, news reporters, and politicians often use teleprompters because they allow the speaker to maintain eye contact and connection with the audience. This strategy engages students by asking them to create the content that will be used with a make-believe teleprompter.

■ Step by Step

1. Place students in groups of three to four. Each of the students will have a specific role in the creation of the teleprompter content.

2. Provide students with an overview of the content or with the necessary resources and materials to use during their small group time.

3. Provide students with a specific content, questions, or topics to research during their group time.

4. Student roles could include: a writer/researcher, an editor, a reporter, a producer, or a director. It may be necessary to provide students with specific tasks for each role. It may also necessary for students to serve more than one role.

5. Give students a time frame for which to complete the task of creating a speech that will be given using a teleprompter. Give each group poster board on which to write the speech.

6. During group work time, roam around the room and provide direction to student groups.

7. When all groups have created, edited, and practiced their teleprompter speeches, consider allowing them the chance to present in front of the whole group. If this is the case, help the groups to limit the speeches to 2 to 3 minutes.

■ Tips and Variations

♦ For groups that struggle to determine roles, consider assigning the roles randomly or assign the roles to certain students based on their strengths.

♦ It is permissible, depending on the age and/or ability of the students, to provide them with the actual content or examples that should be included in the speeches. This could be done formally by distributing fact sheets or informally by telling the groups about important facts or examples they should include.

♦ Consider combining **Teleprompter** with **Send-A-Spy**, **Gallery Walk**, or a **Mind Map.**

What Would _____ Say?

■ Overview

This strategy offers students a unique way to look at content or solve a problem by considering the content or problem from the perspective of a famous person.

■ Step by Step

1. Review the objectives of the lesson and provide students with an opportunity to review and consider what they know or understand about the topic.

2. Provide students with the name of a famous personality or provide them with a list of famous names from which to choose.

3. Provide students with time to consider how that famous person would solve the given problem or ask them to think about what that person would say about the content.

4. It may be helpful to provide the students with a list of characteristics of some of the individuals that they have to choose from. For example, the characteristics that may be accurate to describe Shaquille O'Neil could include athletic, persistent, humorous, hard-working, entertaining, etc.

5. Questions can be posed to students in the following ways:

   "How would Shaq describe the _____?"

   "If Oprah Winfrey were a part of this discussion, what would she say?"

   "If the principal wanted to know more about this topic, what questions would she ask?"

■ Tips and Variations

◆ Teachers should avoid naming personalities who may be controversial. Although certain popular athletes and entertainers may provoke the interest of students, the connections students may make may not be appropriate for school.

◆ Considering combining this strategy with **Q and A Match**, **Card Sort**, or a **Fish Bowl**.

◆ Famous personalities can include actors, politicians, historical figures, athletes, scientists, or entertainers. It helps when students have some background knowledge about the individual including important characteristics.

◆ This strategy could be done in conjunction with the reading of a novel or after studying historical events.

Whip Around

■ Overview

This strategy allows students to compare answers in a fun, slightly competitive manner. The **Whip Around** strategy gets students out of their seats and allows them a safe method for comparing answers and getting feedback.

■ Step by Step

1. Place students in pairs, or when necessary, trios.

2. Provide each student with an **Individual Student Whiteboard**, marker, and eraser. If no whiteboards are available, students can use blank sheets of notebook paper with a book or clipboard as a writing surface.

3. Instruct students stand back to back and wait for the question or prompt.

4. After the teacher asks a question (9 x 7 = ?), students write the answer on their board without looking at the boards of other students.

5. When cued, the students turn around ("Whip Around") and compare their answers with the partners.

6. Students erase their answers and return to the back-to-back stance and wait for the next question or prompt from the teacher.

■ Tips and Variations

♦ Consider grouping reluctant or struggling learners with students who have a solid grasp on the content or allow them to be part of a trio where they consult with each other before writing down the answer.

♦ For students who struggle to behave in an appropriate manner, have them participate without a partner.

♦ Consider combing **Whip Around** with **Partner Pretest** or **Yup, Nope, Maybe**.

Yup, Nope, Maybe

■ Overview

With apologies to the grammar police, this strategy offers students a fun and low-stress opportunity to self-reflect on their understanding of key ideas in the lesson.

■ Step by Step

1. Provide students with a listing of the key ideas, terms, or concepts from the lesson. The listing can be on a board or projector.

2. Instruct students that they will be working with partners to consider their understanding of some of the key ideas being learned.

3. Tell students that when their partner shows or tells them a word, they will respond with either a "Yup," "Nope," or "Maybe."

4. A response of "Yup" will indicate that the student can define or give an example of the term. A response of "Maybe" will indicate that the student is unsure but could attempt a definition. A response of "Nope" will mean that the student does not have a clear understanding of the concept.

5. Lead students to work with their partners to respond to each term listed. Students should take turns in order to allow each student to reflect on their own understanding.

6. Ask students to record or divide the words into three stacks corresponding to how each student responded.

7. For those terms in the nope and maybe stacks, ask students to discuss the words, locate definitions, or find examples.

■ Tips and Variations

♦ For those teachers who prefer more proper grammar, students can indicate with a yes, no, maybe.

♦ Consider combing **Yup, Nope, Maybe** as a follow up to a **Rank It** or in combination with **Flash Cards 2.0**.

♦ **Critical Thinking Connection**—Lead students to select words or terms that are in the Yup category and challenge them to evaluate or rate their level of confidence with each term. For those concepts that students rate low, ask them to create a visual representation of the ideas or create a story that utilizes the ideas.

Part Six

Strategies for Student Movement

Ball Toss

■ Overview

This strategy offers a fun, novel way to help students to summarize the learning and to discover the ideas and thoughts of other students in the class. Students are asked to toss a ball or other small, soft object around the room and share their ideas as well as repeat back the ideas and examples of other students in the class.

■ Step by Step

1. Invite students to sit on their desks or stand around the room.

2. Remind students of the content being studied and ask them to think for a few minutes about the important things they've learned. If needed, allow students to use an **MIP**, or **My Top 10 List** as a reference.

3. Give one student a soft ball (one that is easy to catch and won't do damage if it hits a student in the head)

4. Ask that first student to say a term, example, or idea from the lesson.

5. Instruct that student to toss the ball to another student who repeats what the first person said and adds another idea.

6. Continue the **Ball Toss** until all the students have caught, passed, and added an idea.

■ Tips and Variations

♦ Students could also start over from the beginning if the ball hits the ground. This adds the element of repetition to the activity.

♦ Keep this activity fun and light-hearted since students will vary in the ability to catch and toss. Avoid allowing students to become overly competitive and remind them that the strategy is called **Ball Toss**, not Ball Throw.

♦ **Critical Thinking Connection**—An option is to have students ask a question of another student before they toss the ball. The student who catches the ball answers the question and then poses another question for a different student.

Change of Perspective

■ Overview

For some students, learning is highly correlated to their physical position and place in the classroom. In some learning environments, students are asked to sit for extended periods of time resulting in only one physical perspective of the learning and activities in the classroom. This strategy offers students the chance to change physical locations in the room in order to repeat information or extend their learning.

■ Step by Step

1. Pose a question, example, or problem to students and ask them to consider a response.

2. Have students stand up and push in their chairs.

3. Tell students that when they are given a signal, they will move to another spot in the classroom. That other spot could be another student's desk, near a wall, or on the floor.

4. When students are in their new locations, have them think again about the question, example, or problem that was posed. If appropriate, provide additional instruction or re-teaching of important concepts.

5. Tell students that part of learning is repetition but that it also helps to repeat the learning in different ways and in different locations.

6. After students have had time to repeat and share information in their new location, ask them to return to their original seats and repeat the information one more time.

■ Tips and Variations

◆ If children are asked to sit at another student's desk, offer them the opportunity to leave a note with a positive message, a key idea, or a summary of what they learned while at that desk. This helps when it is time for students to transition back to their own seats because they'll have a special message or note waiting for them.

◆ This strategy can be easily combined with **Individual Student Whiteboards**, **Voting Stickers**, or **Choral Response.**

Consultation

Overview

The power of this strategy lies in the fact that students are provided the opportunity to be an expert or a "consultant" and get the chance to provide advice and suggestions for their "client."

Step by Step

1. Have students form pairs and sit knee to knee.

2. Tell students that one of the partners is going to be the expert/consultant and the other is going to be the client/customer. Based on the age of the students, provide examples of experts and the role they play. For example, help students to understand that a medical doctor plays the role of an expert in the field of health and medicine and people seek out their advice when they are sick.

3. The client starts by asking a question of the expert such as, "When I write using the business letter format, I get stuck remembering which comes first. Can you help me figure out a way to remember that?"

4. The consultant then helps the client with ideas and suggestion to solve the problem.

5. After students have had sufficient time to discuss their problem or scenario, ask students to switch roles and pose another problem, question, or scenario.

Tips and Variations

♦ If the room set up allows, students could sit on the floor or stand with their partners.

♦ Some reluctant and shy students may benefit from the use of **Sentence Starters** to help them start the conversation.

♦ For some students, the teacher can simply provide the topic (steps in the scientific process, for example). For others, the teacher may need to provide the actual problem/question to discuss as well as possible solutions that could be offered by the "consultant."

♦ Consider combining **Consultation** with **Yup, Nope, Maybe**, **Journal Response**, or **Rank It**.

Corners

■ Overview

This strategy offers a quick and effective movement break and allows students the opportunity to share their ideas in an informal setting. Corners are defined as designated areas of the classroom where students go to share their ideas.

■ Step by Step

1. Prior to the lesson, create posters and place them around the room. Types of posters could include modes of transportation, vacations spots, famous people, or types of food. The content of the posters do not necessarily need to relate to the content being studied.

2. When cued, ask students to stand and walk to the corner/poster of their choice.

3. Once the students are at the corner/poster of their choice, provide them with a quote, question, or topic.

4. After students have had time to think about their response, ask them to share their ideas with students who are next to them at the Corner.

5. Example—"Students, we have just spent several minutes determining cause and effect in the story. We all need a quick stretch break. Everyone please stand. Look around the room and locate the posters that have types of animals on them. We have a poster with a bear, one with a lion, one with a squirrel, and another with a turtle. When I say go, please go stand next to the one of the animal posters. You may pick whichever one you like."

■ Tips and Variations

♦ For larger classes, it is helpful to have the students form pairs or trios once at the corner of their choice.

♦ **Corners** can be combined with **What Would _____ Say**, **Change of Perspective**, or **My Top 10 List**.

♦ Some teachers prefer to ask students to bring books, handouts, or other materials to their **Corner** in order to have a resource to support the discussion.

♦ **Critical Thinking Connection**—Place specific questions or quotes on the back or next to the posters in each corner. When students arrive at the corner, ask one student to read the question. Lead students at that corner to discuss the question. The questions or quotes can also be differentiated based on student ability level or interest.

Create-A-Skit

■ Overview

Students are often motivated by the opportunity to act out their understanding of the content being learned. Skits, role plays, and acting appeal to a variety of students and the **Create-A-Skit** strategy offers many different tasks and roles that students can play. This strategy offers students the chance to both deepen their understanding and also correct any misconceptions.

■ Step by Step

1. Provide students with an overview of the big ideas and major objectives of the lesson or unit.

2. Place students in pairs or small groups and instruct them that they'll be working together to **Create-A-Skit** of between 30 seconds and 2 minutes that will highlight an important concept, event, problem, or fact being learned.

3. When students are in their groups, provide different roles that each person can play. For example, each partner could be an actor in the skit or one person can direct, another can write, another can edit or work on props. However, each member of the group should be knowledgeable of the final skit and be able to communicate how the skit relates to the learning.

4. Provide time for the groups to create, practice, and rehearse their skits.

5. If appropriate, provide time for the groups to present their skit to their peers. This can be done in front of the whole group, in smaller groups, or on video.

6. After the skits have been created and performed, ask students to summarize and expand their understanding by responding in a **Journal**.

■ Tips and Variations

♦ It is not necessary for each group to always present their skit to the whole class. Part of the power of **Create-A-Skit** is in the involvement in the creative process, not necessarily in the performance.

♦ Consider combing **Create-A-Skit** with a **Mind Map, Concept Collage**, a **Quick Write**, or **What Did You *Hear*?**

♦ **Critical Thinking Connection**—Inexpensive props such as hats, scarves, and clothing can add a more interactive element to the skits. Challenge students to consider which props, materials, or images best convey important messages.

Dueling Flip Charts

■ Overview

Typically used as a culminating activity, this strategy divides students into two groups in order to compete to see which team can complete an acrostic related to the content. It is typically high energy and leaves students feeling good, laughing, and eagerly looking to see what their team was able to accomplish.

■ Step by Step

1. Prior to the lesson secure chart paper and markers.

2. Brainstorm key terms, words, or ideas that are related to the content.

3. Choose a key term or phrase that is important for students to remember.

4. Use that key term or phrase to create an acrostic that will be written vertically down the left hand side of the chart paper. Write the same information on each chart. For example, for a science class studying Pangaea, vertically write the word Supercontinent down the left hand side of the charts.

5. Divide the class into two teams.

6. Have students line up single file in front of each chart and give the first student in each line a marker.

7. When cued, the first student races up to the chart and writes a word related to the unit of study that begins with one of the letters in the term *Supercontinent*. For example, they may write *earth* next to the letter *e* or *crust* next to the letter *c*.

8. The marker is then handed to the next person in line who then races up to the chart to complete another letter in the acrostic. This process is repeated until all students have had the chance to add an idea. The first team to complete the acrostic wins.

9. When both teams have completed their charts, show the entire class what both groups completed and look for commonalities.

■ Tips and Variations

♦ If there are concerns about the noise level and/or ability of certain students to maintain self-control during **Dueling Flip Charts**, divide the class into several teams with fewer students in each team.

♦ Allow each team a "coach" whose job it is to help the team by reminding them what letters still need to be completed. Their job is not to provide answers but say things like, "We still need to think of something to go with the letter t."

♦ Allow the right to pass if students can't think of something to add to the chart.

Gallery Walk

■ Overview

Students who participate in this strategy get the benefit of physical movement combined with sharing of information with a partner. It is often used as a review or summarization technique but it can also be adjusted and used when students are first exposed to a topic.

■ Step by Step

1. Prior to a lesson or unit, create 5 to 10 questions, comments, quotes, or scenarios that relate to the objective(s) of the lesson. Write those on chart paper and post them around the room.

2. Instruct students in the manner and method you'd like them to follow when participating in the **Gallery Walk**. (Alone or with partners? Specific route or go in any order they prefer?)

3. Provide students specifics regarding how much time they'll have and what specific tasks they need to complete during the walk.

4. When cued, ask students to begin the **Gallery Walk**. While students are walking to the posters and discussing the questions with partners, walk around the room in order to check student understanding and answer student questions. This also offers a good opportunity to discover which questions or topics are most difficult for students to comprehend or explain.

5. When the **Gallery Walk** is complete, ask students to return to their desks and share with partners or do a **Picture This**, a **Mind Map**, or **Flash Cards 2.0**.

■ Tips and Variations

♦ This strategy can also be used when students have completed independent work. They can either chose a partner for a **Gallery Walk** with or they can chose to go alone.

♦ Some teachers prefer to ask students to follow a predetermined path or order while doing the **Gallery Walk**. However, depending on the space available in the room and the number of students walking at the same time, students could choose the order so long as they visit to each poster.

♦ One option is to ask students to complete a "super" **Gallery Walk** by reviewing the posters in a timed manner. This option works well with students who are reviewing topics that need to become automatic such as math facts.

♦ Some teachers prefer to offer students the chance to carry a clip board to record answers or complete tasks while conducting the **Gallery Walk**.

♦ The use of a visual timer is helpful during this strategy.

Give One/Get One

■ Overview

This strategy allows for movement, social interaction, and the exposure to many different ideas. Its strength lies in the fact that students get to move around the room to learn about the perspectives, ideas, and thoughts of other students.

■ Step by Step

1. Provide each student with a Post-It Note, 3x5 card, or a piece of paper.

2. Give the students a prompt, question or topic to write about and provide them with thinking and writing time.

3. Instruct students to write a brief response that is legible because others students will be reading it.

4. After students have completed their written response, have them stand.

5. Instruct students that when cued they will move around the room and share responses with several others students. It is also helpful to tell students the number of times they will share information with partners.

6. After partners have shared their responses with partners, *they trade cards* so each partner has a new card (they give one and get one!)

7. The students then find new partners and share the information/answer from *the card they are currently holding,* not their original response. Students will give one and get one each time they share with a partner.

8. When students have completed giving one and getting one, ask them to return to their seats and discuss with partners what they learned.

■ Tips and Variations

♦ Like many movement strategies, it is crucial for **Give One/Get One** to be clearly modeled for students. In addition, it is often helpful to do a fun topic or question before students are asked to share content-based topics. For example, students could list the name of their favorite childhood toy.

♦ If students struggle to transition from one partner to the next, instruct them to raise their hand when they are done with one partner. When they notice another person with their hand raised, they become partners.

♦ In smaller groups, it is possible for students to get their original response back at some point. In that case, merely tell the students to share what they have since they'll get an additional idea with the next partner.

♦ This strategy could be combined with a **Card Sort**, **Rank It**, or **My Top 10 list**.

Hand Motions

■ Overview

Hand Motions are similar to **Response Cards** except that students show or demonstrate understanding using their hands or body motions. It provides a quick movement activity for students and gives the teacher an opportunity to quickly assess the understanding of the class.

■ Step by Step

1. Review key concepts from the lesson and allow students with time to think about their knowledge.

2. Pose a question to students that can be answered using a hand motion.

3. Demonstrate to students the types of **Hand Motions** or movements that can be used to represent their choices, ideas, or thoughts.

4. Provide wait time and, if appropriate, ask students to consult with a partner to consider their answer.

5. When given a signal, instruct students to display their **Hand Motion** to indicate their response to the question.

■ Tips and Variations

◆ Some teachers prefer to ask students to keep their **Hand Motions** private so that other students don't rely on the votes/motions of their peers. In this case, ask students to display their **Hand Motions** at chest level instead of above their heads.

◆ Some students will delay showing their **Hand Motion** response and prefer to look around the classroom for confirmation or correction from their peers. In many cases this is appropriate and developmentally necessary. In that case, allow students the opportunity to talk with their partners either before or after they show their **Hand Motion**.

◆ Examples of **Hand Motions** include Thumbs Up/Thumbs Down, using fingers to represent different choices such as A, B, C, or D, and sign language to represent and idea.

Inside/Outside Circle

■ Overview

This strategy offers students a quick and fun way to share or expand their ideas with other students in the class. In addition to physical movement, students are given the opportunity to listen to other students, provide feedback, and answer questions.

■ Step by Step

1. Have students stand and form two circles, one smaller inside and one larger one outside. Each circle should have the same number of participants, if possible.

2. The inner circle will have students stand closer—shoulder to shoulder. Students on the inside circle face outward and outside circle faces inward.

3. Each student should be standing directly in front of a partner. (If there is an odd number, one trio will be fine.)

4. Provide the students with a question, problem, or scenario to discuss and provide think time.

5. When cued, the partners discuss or share.

6. When it is time to move, direct either the inside or outside circle to move and how many spaces or partners to move. For example, the teacher might say, "The outside circle only, move three people to your left."

7. When the students have new partners, pose a new question or scenario.

■ Tips and Variations

♦ If the physical space in the classroom does not permit two circles, students can form two lines, each facing each other. When it is time to rotate partners, the end of each line will need to shift sides in order to avoid bunching up at one end.

♦ Like most strategies with multiple steps, it may take several practice attempts before students become proficient.

♦ If students have trouble maintaining circles or figuring out how to rotate, consider having them sit on the floor after they have formed circles.

♦ **Coded Reading** can be used prior to this strategy to provide students with specific content/topics to discuss. Students should be encouraged to bring books, materials, notes, or "cheat sheets" to aide their discussions.

♦ Consider following this strategy up with a **Journal Response** or **Circle, Triangle, Square** strategy to further cement the learning.

Line Ups

■ Overview

At a moment's notice, this simple strategy can be used to help students make a decision, consider choices, or to simply discover what others in the class think about a topic.

■ Step by Step

1. Prior to the lesson, prepare three to five statements that require students to make a choice or to express an opinion.

2. Have students stand and instruct them that when they are given a cue, they'll walk to one side of the room or another depending on their opinion about the topic or prompt.

3. Make a statement and ask students to choose a side of the line.

4. Once students have lined up, ask them to share their ideas with a partner or call on a student to share why they lined up where they did.

5. Example—After reading and discussing a short story, ask students to line up to express their opinion to statements such as, "The most important thing to happen to the main character was _____. If you totally agree, stand on that side of the room. If you totally disagree, stand on the other side of the room. If you are not sure, you can stand somewhere in the middle. If you are leaning one way, but are not 100% in agreement, you can stand between that side and the middle."

■ Tips and Variations

♦ Depending on the class make up and how comfortable students are agreeing or disagreeing with their peers, ask them to first think about their response and then, when cued hold up the number of fingers showing their opinion before they move to a side of the room.

♦ It is permissible to allow students to change their opinions based on what others in the class have said.

♦ Consider combing **Line Ups** with **MIP**, **2 Truths and a Lie**, or **Unique Idea Only**.

♦ **Critical Thinking Connection**—Challenge students to place themselves in the role of another student, another historic personality, or to consider the **Line Up** statement from a different perspective.

Move and Touch

■ Overview

The simple act of standing and moving around the room can be energizing and fun for students. This strategy takes no preparation and students never tire of it. It offers students the chance to move, practice positive social interactions, and share information.

■ Step by Step

1. Ask students to stand and push in their chairs.

2. Tell students to take a second and think about the content that is currently being studied. For example, "Students, we have just spent the last 15 minutes practicing triple digit addition. Please take a second and think about your progress in mastering that skill."

3. Tell the students that when they are given a signal, they will move around the room and touch several physical objects. For example, "Students, when I say go, move around the room and touch 6 objects with a right angle."

4. When students have touched the last object, instruct them to stop right where they are.

5. Have students find partners with a person standing closest to them.

6. Provide students with a question, scenario or problem related to the objective and ask students to share with their partners.

7. When students are finished sharing, have them go back to their seats and continue their work.

■ Tips and Variations

♦ **Move and Touch** can take anywhere between 30 seconds and 5 minutes depending on the needs of the students.

♦ Students can do several rounds of moving, each time touching different types of objects and working with different partners.

♦ Consider combining Move and Touch with **Corners**, **What Did You _Hear_**, **Word Splash**, or an **I Learned Chain**.

Snowball Fight

■ Overview

This high-energy strategy combines fun, the chance to throw paper, and the ability to review the ideas and comments of other students. Often used as a culminating activity, it can also be used for students to pose questions to each other or provide examples, definitions, or problems.

■ Step by Step

1. Provide each student with a half sheet of paper.

2. Remind students of the key objectives of the lesson and provide them with time to think about what they know about the topic.

3. Pose a question to students and ask them to write the answer on the half sheet of paper.

4. Once all students have written their response, have them crumple the paper into a ball (snowball).

5. Have students stand, push in their chairs, and hold on to their snowballs.

6. Divide the class into two teams and provide boundaries that each team must stay within.

7. Instruct students that when they are cued, they will be given 1 minute to have a **Snowball Fight**. During that time they are to constantly collect and throw snowballs at the other team.

8. When time is up, have each student collect one snowball and read what is written on it. They can share that information with partners or compare it to what they wrote on their own snowball.

■ Tips and Variations

♦ If the teacher is concerned that some students won't act appropriately while throwing the snowballs, one alternative is to take a box, empty trashcan, or other target and place it in the middle of the room. When cued, have students throw their snowballs at the target instead of at each other.

♦ An option is to have students throw the snowballs in the air or at an arc instead of directly at another person.

♦ This strategy works well when students are asked opinion-based questions rather than fact-oriented ones that have only one correct answer.

♦ Consider combing a **Snowball Fight** with **Create the Test**, **Unique Idea Only**, or a **Quick Write**.

Stand When

Overview

This is perhaps the simplest of all the movement strategies but also one of the most effective. Students are simply given an opportunity to stand as a means of showing agreement, expressing readiness, or as a way to respond to a prompt.

Step by Step

1. Remind students of the key concepts and topics being studied.

2. Pose a question and provide think time.

3. Instruct students that when they are cued, they will stand to respond to the question.

4. Repeat the question and instruct students to **Stand When** they feel they have an answer to the question.

5. Once all or most students are standing, ask them to share their idea with a partner.

6. Example—"Students, we have been discussing why the Colonies wanted to break away from England. Think about the reasons we discussed. Stand when you have an answer in your mind."

Tips and Variations

♦ Remind students that not everyone is expected to stand at the same time.

♦ After students are standing, they can use fingers to represent the strength of confidence in their answer. For example, students could hold up eight, nine, or ten fingers if they are very confident in their answer or one to three fingers if they are not very sure of their answer. Students could then partner up to share their ideas.

♦ Some students may not want to stand for fear of embarrassment or being called on to talk to the whole class. In that case, it is appropriate to tell the students that they won't be called on just because they stand up. The act of standing is merely to indicate that a student has an idea.

Voting Stickers

■ Overview

Students of all ages enjoy getting stickers on their assignments. This strategy turns the table and uses stickers as a way for students to express their ideas and opinions.

■ Step by Step

1. Prior to the lesson, place key words, concepts, or terms from the unit of study on posters around the room.

2. Provide each student with an equal number of stickers or small Post-It Notes.

3. Instruct students that they will vote by placing their stickers according to the question or topic that will announced.

4. When cued, students take their stickers and place them in a designated area on the poster according to the question that was posed.

5. Example—"Students, think about the persuasive paper we've been writing. In just a moment, you are going to vote by placing your stickers on the posters around the room. The first thing I want you to think about is the purpose or reason we write in a persuasive style. Everyone stand and go place your sticker on the poster that has the best reason or definition to the question about why we write in a persuasive style."

■ Tips and Variations

♦ The information from the **Voting Stickers** can be charted and graphed in order to provide a visual representation of student knowledge.

♦ Consider using the same questions and **Voting Sticker** activity as both a pre-lesson and a post-lesson assessment. This can be helpful in demonstrating to students how much they have learned.

♦ Other options for voting include: item most likely to be on a test, the most difficult to explain to another person, easiest to solve, or the one with the most examples.

♦ Consider combining **Voting Stickers** with **Gallery Walk**, **Move and Touch**, or **Consultation**.

Wear-A-Word

Overview

Students benefit from consistent exposure to words, topics, and concepts. In addition to exposure, this strategy offers students a fun and novel way to use and practice words associated with the concept being studied.

Step by Step

1. Provide each student with a sticky name tag, envelope-type sticky labels that go on folders or stickers that are large enough to write on.

2. Ask students to think about key words, terms, or topics that are related to the lesson.

3. Instruct students to write a term, word, or example on the stickers or name tag and place them on their sleeves.

4. Have students stand move around the room with the purpose of reading the words or ideas that other students are wearing.

5. Example—Provide students with a list of vocabulary words that will be learned or encountered during the unit of study. Ask each student to select one word and write it on their name tag. After students have placed their sticker on their arm or sleeve, instruct them to walk around the room and when cued, pair up with another student. Students could be asked to share one or two things they know about the term, give a synonym or antonym, or use the term in a sentence.

Tips and Variations

♦ Plastic name tag holders (the type that are handed out at workshops and conferences) also work great for this activity.

♦ Consider combing **Wear-A-Word** with **Change of Perspective**, **Quick Write**, or **Yup, Nope, Maybe**.

♦ **Critical Thinking Connection**—Give each student a term but do not let them see what it is. Place the term on their back. As students mill around the room, their partners see what term is on their back and give them clues in order to help them guess the word. The power of this approach is in giving the clues, not in guessing the correct answer.

Part Seven

Bonus Strategies for Reluctant Learners

"Reluctant learners are reluctant for a reason."
—Kirsten Olson

The following strategies are designed for those "still-reluctant" learners who struggle to participate in classroom activities because of inappropriate behaviors, lack of self-confidence, or other issues that prevent them participating in a positive manner with their peers. Unlike the previous strategies, these are designed to be implemented in one-on-one or small group settings.

When working with reluctant students, it is important to remember that all behaviors happen for a reason. That is, students are reluctant for a reason. They may lack positive role models, they may not fully understand the expectations, they may expect to be ridiculed or teased by classmates, they may just be shy, or they may have a learning disability. Regardless of why a student is reluctant to participate in classroom activities, the effective teacher utilizes specific methods and strategies that encourage participation while building student skill and confidence.

It is important not to confuse reluctance to participate with motivation to learn. In fact, many of our most reluctant students are very motivated to learn. Some students are only reluctant to learn in the *school* setting. Eric Jensen, author of *Teaching with the Brain in Mind*, reminds us that, "...the human brain loves to learn: Our very survival, in fact, is dependent upon learning." For teachers who wish to work effectively with reluctant learners, they must help students build the skills and confidence that will enable them to be productive members of the class.

Working with reluctant learners can be a challenge and teachers should not expect immediate, overnight results. Although some students will respond quickly to these strategies, helping students build the necessary skills can take time. The strategies on the following pages have a few important characteristics in common:

- ♦ They allow reluctant learners the chance to maintain control and choice. The strategies avoid direct attempts at controlling or manipulating behavior.

- ♦ They help to build relationships with students and open lines of communication that allow for feedback and ideas to be exchanged between the student and teacher.

- ♦ They express positive intentions and belief that the student can and will participate in a positive manner. It is important to always maintain enthusiasm and hope when working with reluctant learners.

- ♦ They allow reluctant students the safety to participate without the worry of embarrassment or being called upon unexpectedly. They rely on the knowledge that success builds confidence and motivation.

A Head Start

■ Description

We all like to get something for free. We all like the feeling of getting just a little bit more than what we paid for. Who hasn't been drawn into one of those *buy one, get one free* sales?

There are marketing experts and psychologists who study the art of persuasion who wonder why this is and why it is such a powerful force. Beyond the obvious answer, "Because you *get* something," experts want to know how this process works. Researchers from the University of Pennsylvania conducted an experiment and got some surprising results. It seems that the *perception* of self interest (getting something) is as powerful as actually getting something.

The researchers studied patrons at a car wash. Two groups were identified and each was given a customer loyalty card. One group was given a card where they would receive a free car wash after eight visits. So, for group one, they paid for eight visits and got the ninth free. The second group also got a card but this one required the customers to get ten car washes before they got a free one. The twist was that for the second group, the first two spots were already stamped. It was as if this group had gotten two free car washes. They seemed to have a head start on the first group. But when you compare closely, you'll notice that both groups still had to buy eight car washes in order to get one free. The difference? *Perceived* self-interest.

How might the concept of perceived self interest transfer to working with reluctant learners?

- ♦ Fill in some of the answers on assignments in order to give them **A Head Start**.

- ♦ Allow students to complete certain portions or sections of an assignment.

- ♦ Allow students choice on which problems or sections of an assignment they'd like to complete.

- ♦ If appropriate, permit students to complete an assignment in the order of their choice.

- ♦ Encourage students to complete easier problems first and then ask them to choose which of the more difficult problems to tackle next.

Big Word Alert

■ Description

The pace of classroom instruction can sometimes leave shy or reluctant students confused and even more hesitant to participate in classroom activities. In many classrooms, students that are able to quickly respond to teacher questions or requests are seen as the more intelligent, willing, or cooperative. This strategy attempts to level the playing field by giving reluctant students advanced notice and information about important words, terms, or ideas that will be discussed during the lesson.

Prior to a lesson, prepare a **Big Word Alert** listing of key words, terms, or ideas as well as corresponding definitions, characteristics, or examples. Provide the list to the student(s) and explain that you will be using these words or examples during the lesson. Review the words and examples briefly with the student(s) and clarify any difficult pronunciations or concepts. The purpose of this preview is to allow the student(s) an individualized **Sneak Peek** of the content and allow students a chance think about words and to ponder questions they may have about the concepts.

When the lesson begins, instruct the student(s) to place the **Big Word Alert** list on their desks. Since the student(s) have been pre-exposed to the words, encourage them to participate in classroom activities by answering questions or providing examples to their peers.

Students can also use the **Big Word Alert** lists to participate by:

- ◆ Tracking the number of times a word or example is used during the lesson.
- ◆ Tracking the number of times a word or example is listed in a textbook, handout, or other resource.
- ◆ Using the list to create questions about the words.
- ◆ Adding synonyms, antonyms, or examples next to the words on the list.
- ◆ Using the lists to create a **Picture This** illustration or **Flash Cards 2.0**.

Closed Fist

▪ Description

The first step for some reluctant learners is to get them to raise their hand to indicate that they'd like to participate in classroom discussions. This strategy gives the student the chance to participate secure in the knowledge that they will only be called upon if they indicate that they'd like to answer a question or provide a comment. Reluctant students often do not raise their hands or only do so when they think there is no likelihood that they'll be called upon.

Speak with the student privately and let them know that you have devised a system that will allow them to indicate to you when, during a lesson, they are ready and willing to participate. Most classrooms have students, at some point during the lesson, raise their hands to answer questions, provide examples, or to indicate agreement.

The **Closed Fist** strategy requires that the student raise their hand and indicate their confidence on a scale expressed with their fingers. When a student raises their hand with a **Closed Fist**, it is an indication that they do not want to answer the question. This allows them to maintain the appearance of participation. For some students, this ability to "play along" with the class may be the first step in building confidence. If the student raises their hand and holds open five fingers, it is an expression that they have full confidence in their answer and that they would like to be called upon to participate. Showing between one and four fingers can express the scale of their confidence or willingness to participate.

Some teachers have a "no hands raised" policy in their classroom. That is, they call on students randomly or use another method to involve students instead of relying on raised hands. Even in these environments, eager students still typically raise their hands and get called upon more consistently than reluctant students. The **Closed Fist** strategy allows for reluctant students to take the first step to involvement with an understanding that the teacher will respect their wishes.

Some students will remain with a **Closed Fist** for weeks or months until they become comfortable speaking out. In this case, respect the student's wishes but consider using **Planted Questions, Sentence Starters,** or **A Head Start** as a way to encourage their participation.

Extend An Invitation

■ Overview

Just about everyone appreciates a genuine invitation to participate in something meaningful or fun. Some students respond to a real, heart-felt invitation by the teacher to participate in the learning task or classroom activities. This strategy relies on a one-on-one conversation between the student and teacher about the importance of participation. However, it doesn't stop at merely inviting a student to participate. It provides the student with specific *ways* to participate.

As an analogy, imagine being invited to a party at someone's home. As you decide if you'll attend, several questions typically go through your mind. *How much do I like this person? Am I available on that day and time? What kind of party is it? Will I be expected to bring anything? Who else will be there? Do I like or dislike any of those people? What will we do at this party?* Although you may not verbalize all of these questions, it is a lot easier to decide to attend if you know some of the answers.

Now imagine the classroom is a bit like a party. In order to decide to attend (or in the case of the classroom, to participate) the student will want to know things like: *What is expected of me? What will I do? What do I do if I don't like what is going on?*

During a one-on-one discussion with a reluctant student the first thing to do is express a genuine concern and desire for the student to participate. It is always more meaningful to get a personalized, genuine invitation. Second, provide the student with a relevant purpose and reason for participating in the classroom activity. Provide them with a certain job or specific task to complete during the lesson. For example, the teacher might ask the student to track the number of times questions were asked, what the average wait time was during questioning, or how often they responded to a student question with a direct answer.

This strategy can be combined with **Planted Questions, The 5-Minute Focus Group**, or **A Head Start**. Just like when a guest leaves your home after a party, it is important to remember to thank the student for their involvement and participation. The expression of appreciation for a job well done can go a long way toward building confidence in reluctant learners.

Looks Like, Sounds Like, Feels Like

■ Overview

Much of the content we teach to students is abstract in nature while many of our students tend to think in more concrete terms. Nowhere is this conflict more evident than the classroom. Teachers often tell students to behave in terms that are abstract and open to interpretation. Students are often implored to *do their best* and *try harder* only to find the teacher's expectations are very different from their own.

Reluctant students may simply need a more concrete way to understand and comprehend teacher expectations. The **Looks Like, Sounds Like, Feels Like** strategy offers teacher and students alike the chance to clarify expectations and state them in concrete terms so that everyone has a clear understanding of what proper classroom participation looks like, what it sounds like, and what it feels like.

Prior to meeting with the reluctant student(s), brainstorm a list of common expectations, statements, and phrases that students might hear in the classroom regarding their behavior and participation. For example, students are often told that they need to study harder, share with their classmates, or use more respectful words. All of these statements assume a common understanding and shared value system. However, all of these statements are open for interpretation. For example, teachers often tell reluctant (or difficult) students to be nicer to their peers. A student could reasonably reply, depending on their background and experiences, "I was being nice, I didn't hit him!"

Provide students with a handout that lists three columns (see Looks Like, Sounds Like, Feels Like on page 133), one labeled Looks Like, another labeled Sounds Like, and another labeled Feels Like. At the top of the sheet, list *one* specific behavior such as working positively with a partner. In partnership with the student(s), brainstorm the specific behaviors that would be expected when students are in that situation. Be as specific as possible. With the above example, students might list *keeping hands to self, sharing supplies such as markers*, and *using words like please and thank you*. The first two columns—Looks Like and Sounds Like—focus on external behaviors that can be seen and measured by both the student and the teacher. The Feels Like column lists how the student would expect to feel if they were meeting expectations. For example, a student might say that they feel *more confident* or *happy* if they were working positively with their peers.

Some teachers have chosen to use this method with the entire class as a way to clarify rules at the beginning of the year.

The 5-Minute Focus Group

■ Description

This strategy is similar to what television show producers and politicians do on a regular basis (with perhaps the difference being the sincerity.) **The 5-Minute Focus Group** allows the teacher to gain valuable insight and feedback from the reluctant student about their perceptions, ideas, and suggestions regarding lessons, instructional strategies, or the classroom environment.

Set aside a few minutes and ask the reluctant student(s) about their opinion of a topic, lesson, or unit that will be taught in the near future. Typically done in private, the purpose of the discussion is to genuinely gauge a student's interest in the topic(s) that will be the focus of the lesson. In addition, seek to gain insight into how the lesson, strategies, or focus can be improved.

For example, the teacher might say, "Tomorrow I will be introducing a lesson on long division. I know that sometimes students struggle to see the importance of long division, especially when we have calculators. I have a few ideas about how I should start the lesson but I'd like to get your ideas. Should I start the lesson by showing a video clip, doing a KWL chart, or by showing examples on the board?"

The teacher should then do their best to incorporate those ideas into the lesson. Depending on the age of the student and their sensitivity to their peers, the teacher could acknowledge the reluctant student's contributions to the class. However, if the lesson is not successful or if it is not well received by the class, avoid publicly acknowledging the student(s) who participated in **The 5-Minute Focus Group**. Regardless of whether or not a student is publicly acknowledged, this strategy helps to build the relationship with the students as well as their confidence that they have valuable ideas to contribute.

The Miracle Question

■ Description

Commonly used in therapy sessions by counselors, **The Miracle Question** helps students to view situations or problems from a different perspective. This strategy can help students to see alternative options for behaviors and help them to create goals and action steps for future behavior.

In a one-on-one setting, pose the following question to the student, "Imagine a time in the future, when by some miracle, _____ is/is not happening." For example, the teacher might ask a reluctant student about their confidence in participating with their peers in small group activities. If the student responds that they don't like to give their ideas because no one will listen to them, the teacher might ask, "Imagine a time in the future, when by some miracle, the other students listened to you and used your ideas. I know it seems like that could never happen, but let's pretend for just a minute. Can you imagine what it would be like to have fun and have your classmates listen to your ideas? What is it like? Describe it for me. What could we maybe do now so that we can get to that point?"

This strategy helps educators to remember that growth is sometimes a slow process for students and they often come to class with other issues or concerns that take precedence over classroom participation. If a student has difficulty imagining how their life or behaviors could be different, consider rephrasing the question with a less sensitive topic. The teacher can also use some humor with this approach by making statements such as, "I know it seems like that could never happen, after all a miracle is something that never seems to happen to us, but it's fun to pretend."

Depending on the teacher-student relationship, and the student's willingness to discuss a topic, the teacher could offer some ideas for the student to think about. The teacher might offer indirect advice such as, "I had a student a couple of years ago who didn't like to participate in small groups either. I didn't blame her because some of the other students were mean to her. Then she tried something that seemed to work and then she started to enjoy small groups. Would you mind if I told you what she did?"

Planted Questions

■ Description

This strategy encourages reluctant students to participate in whole group and small group activities by offering them the opportunity to consider their thoughts, answers, and ideas to questions before they are asked by the teacher. The goal is for the student to become comfortable participating in group discussions with the ultimate aim of giving them the confidence to speak for themselves.

Prior to the lesson, talk privately with the reluctant student(s) and tell them that you have created an easy way for them to participate in class or group discussions. Tell the student the topic of the lesson and then give them a list of the questions that will be asked during the lesson or small group activity. Ask the student to indicate which question(s) they'd like to answer and provide any clarification if needed.

The teacher may also choose to provide the student with a sample **Sentence Starter** that can be used when answering the question. In addition, depending on the confidence level of the student, actual answers or hints may be given to the student. Again, the goal is to build confidence in the student and help them to take the first steps towards positive participation.

Some teachers wonder about the response from other students if they discover that certain students have been given the questions ahead of time. This seems a little like cheating. Furthermore, if the actual answers are also given, it would seem that these students have been given an unfair advantage. It is important to keep in mind that the goal is positive classroom participation, not assessment. The students are not being given answers to test questions nor will they necessarily be given a better grade on any assignment.

The 2x10 Method

■ Overview

The establishment of trusting, sincere relationships with reluctant students is necessary in order for them to thrive in the classroom. This strategy helps to build teacher-student trust through the investment of time and effort on behalf of the teacher. It requires that the teacher invest at least 2 minutes per day for 10 days in a row with the purpose of finding out more about the student.

During this time, the teacher desires to get to know the student's interests, ideas, thoughts, hobbies, and favorite things. Basically, the teacher takes the time to figure out what makes the student tick. It was stated before that reluctant students are reluctant for a reason. **The 2x10 Method** allows the teacher the time to help figure out what is engaging and interesting for the student.

During the 2x10 time, the teacher expresses genuine interest in the student as a person and learner, not just in their progress in a particular subject or their grades in school. In fact, teachers should avoid stressing the importance of grades, behavior, and participation. Students will often see through that obvious trick to manipulate. Instead, make the effort to develop the relationship and find specific things you appreciate and like about the student. Write down positive things about their personality, life experience, or character and share them with the student and their family. Students who feel connected to adults who genuinely care for them are more likely to participate, learn, and grow when they might otherwise want to withdrawal.

As is the case with many of the strategies for reluctant students, notify parents and administrators of your plans and interventions. In all cases, avoid any appearance of impropriety and do this during the school day with the full knowledge and support of the family and administration. It is not necessary that this strategy be done in private, either. Teachers often conduct the 2x10 discussions during passing times, at lunch, while taking students to bus or parent pick up area, or the few minutes before school starts.

Suggested Readings

Abernathy, R., & Reardon, M. (2002) *Hot Tips for Teachers: 30+ Steps to Student Engagement*. Chicago, IL: Zephyr Press.

Allen, R. (2008) *Green Light Classrooms*. Thousand Oaks, CA: Corwin Press.

Bellanca, J. (2009) *200+ Active Learning Strategies and Projects*. Thousand Oaks, CA: Corwin Press.

Beninghof, A. (2006) *Engage ALL Students Through Differentiation*. Peterborough, NH: Crystal Springs Books.

Brassell, D. (2009) *Dare to Differentiate: Vocabulary Strategies for All Students*. San Diego, CA: Academic Professional Development.

Blackburn, B. (2007) *Classroom Instruction from A to Z*. Larchmont, NY: Eye On Education

Campbell, L. (2003) *Mindful Learning: 101 Proven Strategies for Student and Teacher Success*. Thousand Oaks, CA: Corwin Press.

Canady, R., & Rettig, M. (1996) *Teaching in the Block*. Larchmont, NY: Eye On Education.

Darling-Hammond, L. (2008) *Powerful Learning*. San Francisco, CA: Jossey-Bass.

Easton, L. (2008) *Engaging the Disengaged*. Thousand Oaks, CA: Corwin Press.

Ellis, A. (2005) *Research on Educational Innovations*. Larchmont, NY: Eye On Education.

Fredericks, J.A, Blumenfeld, P.S., & Paris, A.H. (2004) *School Engagement: Potential of the Concept, State of the Evidence*. Review of Educational Research (74) 1

Frey, N., Fisher, D., Everlove, S. (2009) *Productive Group Work*. Alexandria, VA: ASCD.

Goodman, G. (1995) *I Can Learn: Strategies for Gray-Area Children*. Peterborough, NH: Crystal Springs Books.

Guillaume, A., Yopp, R., Yopp. H. (2007) *50 Strategies for Active Teaching*. Columbus, OH: Merrill/ Prentice Hall.

Hannaford, C. (2005) *Smart Moves*. Salt Lake City, UT: Great River Books.

Hollas, B. (2005) *Differentiating Instruction in a Whole-Group Setting*. Peterborough, NH: Crystal Springs Books

Hunter, R. (2004) *Madeline Hunter's Mastery Teaching*. Thousand Oaks, CA: Corwin Press.

Jensen, E. (2006) *Enriching the Brain*. San Francisco, CA: Jossey-Bass.

Jensen, E. (2005) *Teaching with the Brain in Mind*. Alexandria, VA: ASCD.

Jensen, E. (2003) *Tools for Engagement*. San Diego, CA: The Brain Store

Lambert, M. & Algozzine, B. (2004) *Strategies That Make Learning Fun.* Longmont, CO: Sopris West Educational Services.

Margulies, N. (2002) *Mapping Inner Space.* Chicago, IL: Zephyr Press.

Marzano, R. (2007) *The Art and Science of Teaching.* Alexandria, VA: ASCD.

Medina, J. (2008) *Brain Rules.* Seattle, WA: Pear Press

Newstrom, J. & Scannell, E. (1998) *The Big Book of Team Building Games.* New York: McGraw-Hill.

Reid, G. (2007) *Motivating Learners in the Classroom: Ideas and Strategies.* Thousand Oaks, CA: Sage Publications.

Ross, E. (1998) *Pathways to Thinking: Strategies for Developing Independent Learners K-8.* Norwood, MA: Christopher-Gordon Publishers.

Rutherford, P. (2008) *Instruction for All Students.* Alexandria, VA: Just Ask Publications.

Silberman, M. (1996) *Active Learning: 101 Strategies to Teach Any Subject.* Needham Heights, MA: Allyn and Bacon.

Smokler, D. (2005) *Making Learning Come Alive.* San Diego, CA: The Brain Store.

Stronge, J. (2002) *Qualities of Effective Teachers.* Alexandria, VA: ASCD

Tate, M. (2003) *Worksheets Don't Grow Dendrites.* Thousand Oaks, CA: Corwin Press.

Tileston, D. (2007) *Teaching Strategies for Active Learning.* Thousand Oaks, CA: Corwin Press.

Tilton, L. (2006) *The Teacher's Toolbox for Differentiating Instruction.* Shorewood, MN: Covington Cove Publications.

Walsh, J., & Sattes, B. (2005) *Quality Questioning.* Thousand Oaks, CA: Corwin Press.

Willingham, D. (2009) *Why Don't Students Like School?* San Francisco, CA: Jossey-Bass.

Willis, J. (2007) *Brain-Friendly Strategies for the Inclusion Classroom.* Alexandria, VA: ASCD.

Wolfe, P. (2001) *Brain Matters: Translating Research into Classroom Practice.* Alexandria, VA: ASCD.

Resources

Strategy Implementation

Self-Reflection Guide

Strategy Name	Date Implemented
What was the goal when implementing this strategy?	
Did this strategy help my students meet the identified goal?	
What went well when implementing this strategy? Why?	
What problems were experienced with this strategy? Why?	
What could be done differently next time to ensure greater success?	
What comments were made by students during the use of this strategy? How might those comments impact the use of this or other strategies?	
Notes (Consider clarity of directions, pacing, time, transitions, materials, and higher order thinking skills.)	

Battling Boredom

Agree

Disagree

Alphabet Summary

A. _____

B. _____

C. _____

D. _____

E. _____

F. _____

G. _____

H. _____

I. _____

J. _____

K. _____

L. _____

M. _____

N. _____

O. _____

P. _____

Q. _____

R. _____

S. _____

T. _____

U. _____

V. _____

W. _____

X. _____

Y. _____

Z. _____

Battling Boredom

Personal Goals

My Goals	My Progress

Rank It

Words	Rank 1-10	Notes

Battling Boredom

Something going around in my mind…

Three things I learned

Something that "squares" with me…

Keepers and Wishers

Keepers	Wishers

Battling Boredom

Date: _____

Dear _____ ,

_____

_____

_____

_____

_____

_____

_____

_____

_____

_____

_____

_____

_____

_____

_____

_____

Sincerely,

_____

Outcome Statements

I was surprised by…

I am clearer about…

I wish I knew more about…

One thing I explain clearly is…

I wonder…

I discovered…

I still want to know…

I learned…

I still don't understand…

I enjoyed…

I plan to…

Something still going around in my mind…

One thing I learned today…

If I were (it/them/him/her) I would…

I would do _____ if…

A question I still have is…

I promise I will…

I am feeling…

One thing I already knew was…

An insight I had…

Something I still don't agree with…

Checklist

To be completed:	Progress:

Coded Reading

 for something they find interesting

 for something they have a question about

 for something they'd like to talk about

 for something that "strikes" them as important

 for a "bright" idea or thought

 for something that "clicks" with them

 for something that reminds them of a task to be completed

 for something that should be repeated

 for something to remember

 for something that is "easy" to do, recall, or recite

Battling Boredom

My Top 10 List

1. _____

2. _____

3. _____

4. _____

5. _____

6. _____

7. _____

8. _____

9. _____

10. _____

Battling Boredom

Common Songs

This Old Man

Twinkle, Twinkle Little Star

Adams Family

Jingle Bells

Old MacDonald

La Cucaracha

Brady Bunch

Frere Jacques

Flintstones

Row, Row, Row Your Boat

Hi Ho, Hi Ho…

London Bridges

She'll Be Comin' Round the Mountain

On Top of Ol' Smokey

Home on the Range

Workin' on the Railroad

The Ants Go Marching

My Bonnie

Battle Hymn

Itsy Bitsy Spider

Bippity, Bopity, Boo

Forced Analogies

"_____ is like a brick wall because…"

"How can _____ be like a pair of glasses?"

"How is _____ similar to a bowl of cereal?"

"How is _____ like an explosion?"

"How is _____ like a car that won't start?"

"_____ is like training a dog because…"

"How can _____ be like a mirror?"

"_____ is most like which of the following modes of transportation?"
   Car, plane, train, or boat?

"_____ is like running a race because…"

"What would a #2 pencil say about this problem?"

"This problem could best be explained by a *bee, rabbit, tiger, or elephant.*"

"A *stapler, ruler, rubber band, or highlighter* would solve this problem by…"

"If _____ had to be solved by a _____, it would…"

Encourage students to create their own forced analogies.

Yes	**No**
True	**False**
Fact	**Opinion**

Sentence Starters

"I am thinking of an example that…"

"The textbook says that…"

"I can think of two examples that show…"

"I think _____ will be…"

"The best example of _____ is…"

"The most important thing to remember about _____ is…"

"I would describe this problem by saying…"

"_____ could be solved by…"

"Based on what I heard, I would suggest that…"

"In my opinion, I would…"

"The best course of action to take would be…"

"I have an idea that is similar to…"

Looks Like, Sounds Like, Feels Like

Topic:		
Looks Like	Sounds Like	Feels Like

— Notes —

— Notes —

— Notes —